A beginner's guide to creating a thriving outdoor space

How to Grow a Garden

Ellen Mary

greenfinch

A beginner's guide to creating a thriving outdoor space

How to Grow a Garden

Ellen Mary

Contents

Introduction 6

CHAPTER 1

THE BASICS

Botany Basics 14
Plant Names Demystified 25
Gardening Terms Explained 31
Why Garden? 37
Top Ten Plants for Wildlife 42

CHAPTER 2

UNDERSTANDING YOUR SPACE

Where to Start 50
Get to Know Your Soil 57
Top Ten Shade-Friendly Plants 62
How Do You Want to Use Your Space? 66
How Much Time Do You Have for Gardening? 70
How to Grow a Lawn 84
Small Space Gardening 88
Top Ten Plants for Balconies 98

CHAPTER 3

SOURCING PLANTS

How to Decode a Plant Label 106
Where to Get Your New Plants 111
What to Look Out For When Buying Plants 115
What Tools Do You Need and
What Are They Used For? 118
How to Grow a Tree 122

CHAPTER 4

PLANTING INTO SOIL

Planting in Pots and Hanging Baskets 130
Top Ten Low-Maintenance Plants 142
How to Make a New Garden Bed 146
Sowing and Growing 152
Top Ten Vegetable Plants 160
How to Grow Herbs 164
What, How and When to Plant 168

CHAPTER 5

KEEPING PLANTS ALIVE

Watering Your Plants 180
Feeding Your Plants 186
Top Ten Edible Flowers 188
How to Deal with Weeds 192
Common Pests and How to Deal With
Them in an Environmentally Friendly Way 196
Top Ten Slug-Resistant Plants 202
Common Plant Diseases and Their Remedies 206
Dead Heading and Pruning 211
How to Make Compost 218
The Gardening Year at a Glance 222

Glossary 230
End Notes 231
Further Reading 232
Index 234
Acknowledgements 239

Introduction

Plants are everything to me, from growing food on my allotment to ornamentals and edibles on my balcony, owning a jungle of houseplants and even eating a plant-based diet. All of these things combine to make one big bundle of joy, every day. I've had this love for plants since I was a child, and to be able to spread the appreciation of plants in my everyday work is a dream come true. I am sure that when you start gardening, you will discover a whole new appreciation for the natural world and a host of wellbeing benefits as you immerse yourself in the world of plants.

Most importantly, throughout your gardening journey remind yourself that your garden does not have to be perfect. Forget TV-show gardens and country-estate lawns. As wonderful as they are, if you have little time, space or inclination, just garden as and when you want to, and let your garden be just how you want or need it to be in order to enjoy it. Try not to feel pressure from your neighbours or from photos in magazines. Take inspiration from the abundance of resources at your fingertips but go your own way and at your own pace. Gardening should be a personal experience as you learn about each plant, the soil and which aspects of gardening appeal to you the most. Go with your own flow.

I have written this book with the environment in mind, from recommending only peat-free compost to advising organic practices. The planet we share with all living creatures is precious, and everything we do has an impact, even if it's just planting up a small window box, which could change a bee's whole world! Your planter might make a neighbour smile as they walk by, it might inspire someone to have a go themselves, but mostly, it should make you happy. From learning which plants are suitable to how to care for your green space, each step will bring you closer to the natural world.

I am vegan and this extends to my gardening practice, which is veganic (organic, no animal products and prevention rather than eradication of pests). So you may notice the omission of some well-used animal-based products or plant feed as you read through this book. I have grown my own food, designed gardens and tended to various gardens and balconies in different countries for many years. I have seen an increase in my crops without the need for animal products. Therefore, I have written this book based on my own gardening experiences. Also, keep in mind that letting go of trying to overly control everything is by far the most holistic way to garden. It benefits you and the environment. Working *with* nature not only vastly improves the biodiversity in your space but it also contributes to your overall wellbeing.

My own gardening habits are a mixture of theory and experimentation, haphazard messiness and obsessive planning. I go with the mood that takes me on the day, season, year – I encourage you to do the same. This book covers the theory; you can dip in and out, as and when the mood takes you, or read it front to back and feel empowered to start growing when you've finished. There is no right or wrong way, and there are no embarrassing questions to ask or failures to be had. No matter how many years anyone has been gardening, things don't always go to plan. In my mind, there really are no 'experts', because there is a never-ending array of new plants, updated science, new technologies and, with more people finding a love of gardening, endless inventive and inspirational ideas. When you garden, you garden for life, and the learning never ends.

So, throw yourself in, get your hands dirty and enjoy the ride. Life is simply better when you are surrounded by plants!

CHAPTER 1

The Basics

This chapter – and in fact the whole book – is designed to make you feel at ease at the prospect of getting out into your garden and fully enjoy doing so. When you start getting your hands in the soil and potting plants, you'll find enjoyment in the activity itself, in nurturing your plants and in the feeling of fulfilment at the results. There is no need to know all of the intricacies of plant life to enjoy a rose blooming or to water your first potted container. There is always a lot of debate from different sides of horticulture as to whether anyone but botanists need to know how plants grow or what the botanical names of each plant are. This chapter covers all of the topics that will help you to discover a deeper connection with plants and a general understanding of the plant kingdom, and how incredible it is. Some of this knowledge may not be needed in day-to-day gardening, but it will help you to fully embrace the plant world and dig a little deeper into how plants grow. If you can take the time to absorb the fascinating way plants have evolved and how they grow from seed to flower or fruit then again seed, it will truly strengthen your relationship with the plants around you and open up a whole world of intrigue and respect.

Botanical names are actually much easier to get to grips with than you might expect and even if you don't use them frequently, knowing a few of the key words will help you – for example, when plant shopping or using plants medicinally. During your gardening journey, you will also come across many horticultural terms and perhaps wonder what on earth they mean! The botanical names and common gardening terms explained in this chapter can be used as a reference as and when you need, so I hope it will provide a basic yet useful guide.

Most significantly of all, gardening is personal to you – it is your space and your choices. Before you embark on your journey, or even if you are in the middle of it, it's helpful to remind yourself of why gardening is so essential for your wellbeing, for the planet and for the community. This chapter will help you to think about what is important to you when you garden.

Botany Basics

Understanding the basics of botany is a really good way to get started with gardening. Of course, you may feel that you want to get on with planting all of the plants that you've spotted and love (and who can resist) but if you take the time to understand a few basic gardening principles, the plants you choose will be more likely to thrive. Besides, understanding how and why plants grow brings us even closer to the natural world, allowing us to observe the intricate and astounding cycle of life, both in the garden and on the planet as a whole.

WHAT IS A PLANT?

Essentially, it's something green and living that photosynthesizes – that's the quick definition. There are many other organisms that also photosynthesize, such as bacteria and algae (which can also be defined as a plant), which are both essential for life on Earth, but for our purposes, we'll focus on land plants. Fungi are also crucial to life on Earth yet they are not actually plants, they make up a whole kingdom in themselves.

On a basic level, a plant consists of roots, stems and leaves, which act as follows:

Roots: these anchor the plant and are usually underground. They absorb nutrients and water from soil, which are needed for the plant to grow.

PLANT HUNTING

There are hundreds of thousands of species of plantae (the kingdom of plants) and humans are always discovering more. Modern-day plant hunters travel our precious planet on quests to discover new species. Some plants are found to have medicinal properties, for example, the recently discovered *Kindia gangan*[1], found in West Africa. This particular species has been studied and found to have potential cancer-fighting properties. Studies are ongoing, but I believe there is a plant to cure every illness – we just have to find them.

Stems: these allow the water and nutrients to reach the leaves, flowers and fruits of a plant. Stems can be found below and above the soil.

Leaves: this is where photosynthesis happens and the food is made to nourish the plant. Leaves are almost always above the soil.

Other characteristics of a plant include flowers, fruit and seeds.

WHAT DO PLANTS NEED?

This is the big question, and the answer often depends on the plant. Remember those diagrams at school about how plants turn the energy from sunlight into nutrients and then emit oxygen? Well, that's where it all starts.

All plants need light, air, moisture, nutrients and space. The level of each of these factors and the growing conditions vary between different species. So, I can't emphasize enough how important it is to read the labels on the plants that you buy (see page 106).

PHOTOSYNTHESIS

Light: can come either from the sun or artificial lighting. Plants use the light energy rather than the heat in order to photosynthesize.

Air: oxygen, nitrogen, carbon dioxide and moisture in the air, along with light energy, allows plants to create glucose and leads to respiration – where sugars and oxygen are turned into energy for plant growth.

Nutrients: nitrogen, phosphorus and potassium are the main nutrients needed, which are broken down in the soil and transported via the water absorbed through the roots to feed the plant.

Space: plants need somewhere for the roots and shoots to grow.

Moisture: water travels to the chloroplasts (organelles found in plant cells) to aid photosynthesis. Plants can't survive without water, but each plant can have vastly different water requirements.

Digging Deeper

When you really think about the process of plant growth, it paints a picture about how important our climate is; how everything is connected and reliant on each other to thrive. Every plant wants to grow, flower, fruit and eventually set seed, ensuring its future survival. Plants are not only sophisticated, but also beautiful, strong, evolutionary, diverse and, in fact, far more resilient than we might imagine – perhaps much more so than humans.

PLANT CLASSIFICATION

At first, this can appear complicated, but for home gardening there is no need to get too in-depth with this – just learning some basic facts will help. The plant kingdom is classified in a few different groups, but the three we will focus on are ferns, gymnosperms and angiosperms, as these are the groups you will mostly enjoy in the garden. Don't be put off by the names, it's actually very easy to pick up the basic information.

Ferns

There are thousands of fern species, from bracken to water fern, but as a home gardener, we know them simply as the feathery foliage plants that thrive in moist shade. As the fronds unfurl in spring they look like aliens emerging from the undergrowth. Ferns are fascinating plants that can be grown in borders or in containers. Even on a shady balcony in hanging baskets they can look truly spectacular. They aren't just green foliage either – ferns can be found in gorgeous rusty colours, purples, silver and various shades of green. You'll often spot ferns in woodlands and on verges in the countryside, where they create a carpet of greenery and habitat for wildlife.

THE FIRST FERNS

As the first plants to conquer the land, ferns command our respect. However, if you have ever had horsetail (*Equisetum arvense*) in your garden, you might recoil in fear. It's an invasive weed that gives gardeners the shivers, yet it's actually in the same classification as ferns (pteridophytes [*tuh-rid-uh-fahyt*] – vascular plants that produce spores) and it has survived 400 million years of life on Earth. No wonder it's so tenacious.

Pteridophytes don't produce flowers, and they produce spores rather than seeds. The reproductive life of these plants is interesting because they already have everything they need. Through various stages of the life cycle they produce their own sperm and egg cells, which eventually grow into a fully grown fern.

TOP FERNS TO GROW

In the garden – scaly male fern (*Dryopteris filix-mas* 'Revolvens'), which is a semi-evergreen fern that will grow in most soils, or painted lady fern (*Athyrium niponicum* var. *pictum*), which has soft green/purple fronds with a silvery effect.

In containers – soft shield fern (*Polystichum setiferum*), which is a soft fern with attractive dropping fronds as they unfurl, or hart's tongue (*Asplenium scolopendrium*), which looks tropical with bright green fronds.

In hanging baskets – lacy autumn fern (*Dryopteris erythrosora* var. *prolifica*), which has lacy dark green foliage that starts out a rusty red colour, or bird's nest fern (*Asplenium nidus*), which is a slow-growing fern that can be grown outside in the summer and inside over winter.

As houseplants – button fern (*Pellaea rotundifolia*) is an easy-to-grow houseplant with dark stems and dark green leaves, or maidenhair fern (*Adiantum raddianum* 'Fragrantissimum'), the 'diva' houseplant with black stems and green triangular fronds.

Gymnosperms

A smaller group than ferns, these mainly consist of plants such as conifers, pines and ginkgo. The seeds of gymnosperms are 'naked', which means they are not enclosed in an ovary or fruit and they don't produce flowers. The seeds are often produced on the leaves, scales or cones and can't be seen until they mature, which is when they are released and carried in the wind or by wildlife.

pine tree

ginko

pine cone

THE PROS AND CONS OF CONIFERS

Pros:
- Mostly evergreen.
- Can grow big and fast (always check the mature height and spread before planting).
- Ideal for privacy.
- Come in all shapes and sizes.
- Work well in mixed borders (check out the planting schemes at gardens such as RHS Wisley and Bressingham Gardens).

Cons:
- Seen as a common plant due to past popularity for hedging.
- Can grow too big if left unmaintained (Leylandii can grow up to 90cm/35in in one year!).
- Take a great deal of water and nutrients from the soil, so it can be difficult to grow other plants around it.

TOP GYMNOSPERMS TO GROW

In the garden – maidenhair tree (*Ginkgo biloba*) is one of the most beautiful of deciduous trees, with green leaves changing to a vibrant yellow in autumn, while Korean fir (*Abies koreana*) has purple cones that turn brown and makes a great outdoor Christmas tree.

In containers – common yew (*Taxus baccata*), with its dark green foliage and bright red berries, is a favourite for formal hedging, while Italian cypress (*Cupressus sempervirens*) is an evergreen with upright branches that look very elegant.

As houseplants – Norfolk Island pine (*Araucaria heterophylla*) has whirly horizontal branches and looks great in a big container, while Japanese juniper (*Juniperus procumbens*) is a compact shrub with trailing branches.

For Christmas – blue spruce (*Picea pungens* var. *glauca*) has the greyish–blue needles recognized as one of the classic Christmas trees, while the Norway spruce (*Picea abies*), with its dark green needles, is one of the most popular of all Christmas trees.

Angiosperms

Gymnosperms and Angiosperms are grouped together and called Spermatophytes (*sper-ma-to-phytes*). Angiosperms differ in a few ways to gymnosperms, but the main difference is that all angiosperms are flowering. By far the biggest and diverse of all land plants, angiosperms are many millions of years old, and different species have evolved to attract pollinators and various other wildlife in many ways, from growing larger stamens for wildlife to see and land on to producing nectar that can only be reached by specific species of wildlife. If you think about the vast changes in climate on Earth over millions of years, it is quite incredible that we have such a huge, thriving variety of flowering plants to enjoy in our gardens and, of course, that includes almost all plants we grow for food.

EVOLUTION IN ACTION

A great example of plant and insect having evolved to mutual benefit is the fig tree (*Ficus carica*) and the parasitic wasp (*Blastophaga psenes*). The wasp enters the fig (the flowers bloom inside) and lays her eggs, which later hatch and disperse the pollen as they leave the fig. It's a perfect partnership. The complexities are much more intricate and incredible, and while technically you do eat wasps when you eat figs, each wasp is only 1.5mm long and the fig is rich in the enzyme ficin, which breaks down the remains of the wasp, so you really don't know it's there!

WHAT IS POLLINATION?

While we can gain immense pleasure from a flower, its natural purpose is to attract pollinators.

Most plants require pollination to take place for reproduction, but not all. Some plants can self-pollinate. Pollen production is all about the everlasting desire that plants have to save their species – not so dissimilar to humans!

Pollination is where the pollen from the male anther is spread to the female stigma. Pollen is transferred mostly by wind and pollinating insects such as bees, hoverflies, beetles, butterflies, ants, moths and many more. Each tiny insect has a role to play in pollinating plants. A bee, for example, visits a plant to collect pollen or nectar. It gets pollen grains all over its body and then flies off to another flower.

ANATOMY OF A FLOWER

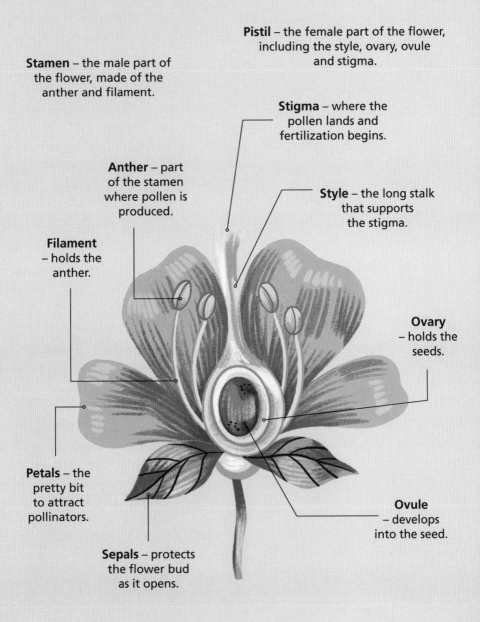

Pistil – the female part of the flower, including the style, ovary, ovule and stigma.

Stamen – the male part of the flower, made of the anther and filament.

Stigma – where the pollen lands and fertilization begins.

Anther – part of the stamen where pollen is produced.

Style – the long stalk that supports the stigma.

Filament – holds the anther.

Ovary – holds the seeds.

Petals – the pretty bit to attract pollinators.

Ovule – develops into the seed.

Sepals – protects the flower bud as it opens.

That pollen gets dropped by accident onto another flower's stigma. The pollen then travels down the style into the ovary where fertilization of the ovules happens, which then grow into seeds. The seeds are, hopefully, given the chance to grow into the next generation of the flowering plant.

Self-pollination is when the pollen from an anther ends up on the stigma of the same flower or another flower on the same plant.

PLANTING FOR POLLINATORS

Pollinators are key to pollinating over 80 per cent of flowering plants, including crops grown for human and animal food production. Hand pollination is often used in breeding new plants and for gardening indoors, but if bees and other insects continue to decline in numbers, food crops will also need to be hand pollinated. The process involves brushing the pollen off one plant with a small paintbrush, then brushing it onto another. It would be an endless task for humankind if we had no natural pollinators left. When you plant for pollinators, you are ensuring that essential wildlife can continue to thrive and crops continue to help feed the world. (See Top Ten Plants for Wildlife, page 42).

Plant Names Demystified

Do you need to know Latin to enjoy gardening? I see the answer as unequivocally 'no, you don't'. There's not many of us who learned Latin in school and this is most definitely not a Latin lesson, but I do find its use in botanical classifications immensely interesting, astoundingly clever and useful for the home gardener – but not essential. All plants have common names, which have lovingly (or not) been given to them based on appearance, use, colour or some other defining characteristic.

FUNNY NAMES

There are so many humorous common names that always seem easier to remember than the Latin. Here are some great examples:

Kangaroo paws (*Anigozanthos flavidus*): look just like fluffy kangaroo paws!

Buzz buttons (*Acmella oleracea*): have yellow and red button-shaped flower heads that numb your mouth when eaten.

Sensitive plant (*Mimosa pudica*): the leaves are so sensitive to touch, they fold inwards.

Sausage tree (*Kigelia africana*): has hanging fruits that look like hot dogs.

Sticky willy (*Galium aparine*): a weed that sticks to clothing.

Corpse flower (*Amorphophallus titanum*): takes ten years to flower, and when they finally do, the scent of the flowers smells like rotting flesh.

As well as having a potentially humorous aspect, common names can cause confusion, as there is some crossover and differences between countries. For example, the common name 'goose grass' is used in other countries for the grassy weed *Eleusine indica*, but in the UK it is used for *Galium aparine* (more widely known as 'cleavers'). If you are recommending a plant, researching a plant or thinking of using it medicinally, knowing the Latin name can help ensure it's the right plant for the right situation. I have frequently been told by friends how excited they are about planting marigolds with tomatoes for pest control, yet having then seen the photos, have noticed that the plants are actually *Calendula* rather than *Tagetes*. Both are both known as marigolds (*Calendula* is more commonly known as pot marigold), but have entirely different uses in the garden and medicinally, and are different species altogether. *Tagetes patula* (French Marigold) is the plant particularly good for pest control. Therefore, it is useful to know the Latin names as it helps to avoid confusion and is the plant language of the world – one commonality we all share!

So, this guide aims to provide a simple explanation of botanical nomenclature, which is the scientific system used to name plants. You don't need to know it all, but an overview can be really helpful. Don't worry about the pronunciation of a Latin name – they vary according to many factors, and there's no need to feel embarrassed if you pronounce a name differently to the next person. It can even be argued that there isn't a correct way of pronouncing any botanical Latin word at all[2] and it can be confusing for professional horticulturalists too.

WHAT'S IN A NAME?

Plant names are broken down into components as follows:

Family – this is the main grouping of plants with similar physical characteristics. There are hundreds of plant families. For example, the family Asteraceae includes plants with daisy-shaped flowers such as sunflowers, dahlias and dandelions. The family Iridacea includes iris, gladiolus and crocus.

Genus – this is the 'generic' name. The genus is a group of related plants. Each genus is part of the higher family group. For example, roses (*Rosa* in Latin) are all part of the family Rosaceae, which also includes plants such as pears and apples!

Species – this is the 'specific' name. It describes one kind of plant within the genus. The species name is usually an adjective and it will most likely refer to something such as the colour, shape or texture. For example, the beautiful, bee-attracting *Digitalis purpurea,* known as the Foxglove, is the genus *Digitalis* and the species *purpurea*, which describes its purple colour.

iris

gladiolus

crocus

Variety – this refers to a version of a plant that is naturally occurring and has not been bred by humans. It is usually the name after the abbreviation: var.

Cultivar – a type of plant specifically bred by humans. Each species can have lots of cultivars, as breeders continue to cultivate plants with advantages to gardeners. For example, disease- and pest-resistant plants, even colours and textures can be bred specifically. This is usually written after the abbreviation: cv; or within single quote marks.

Other Terms You Might See

× – the '×' in a plant name shows that it is a cross between two different species. For example: *Digiplexis × valinii* 'Illumination Apricot', which is a hybrid foxglove and the result of cross-breeding a *Digitalis purpurea* with an *Isoplexis canariensis,* resulting in a much hardier plant.
f. – a plant with a slight difference to the species
supsb. – a subspecies has a particular variant
tm – the name is branded and cannot be reused
(PBR) – plant breeders rights (intellectual property)
PVR – plant variety protection (another intellectual property right for breeders)

WHAT DO PLANT NAMES MEAN?

When you read plant names, having a few hints about what each word means can be incredibly useful for learning their characteristics. We already know that *purpurea* is purple, so you can see that some words are similar to the English word. If you are buying a young plant with no photo, then knowing what the plant label means will help to show you what it will look like when it matures.

Here are some common Latin descriptive words you might find on plant labels:

Colour
alba – white
argentea – silver
aureus – gold
cyaneus – bright blue
luteus – yellow
rosea – rose
rubrum – red
violaceus – violet
viridis – green

Scent
aromatica – aromatic
foetida – foul fragrance
fragrantissima – highly fragrant
graveolens – unpleasant, strong
            fragrance
odorus – fragrant
suaveolens – sweet fragrance

Foliage
lactifolia – broad leaves
macrophylla – large leaves
maculata – spotted
microphyllus – small leaves
palmatum – palm shaped
sempervirens – evergreen
serrata – serrated
variegata – variegated

Flower
campanulata – bell shape
floribunda – free flowering
galeate – hooded
grandiflora – large
plena – double
spicata – spiky
tubulate – tubular

Growth
arborea – tree/branching
contorta – twisted
fruticosa – shrubby
globosus – globe
horizontalis – horizontal growing
magna – large
nana – small
pendula – weeping
repens – creeping

globosus

variegata

Origins

africana – Africa
canadensis – Canada
chinensis – China
japonica – Japan
occidentalis – West to North America
orientalis – East Asia
sibirica – Siberia

Other

alpinus – alpine
maritima – coastal
mollis – soft
montana – mountains
officinalis – medicinal use
pratensis – meadow
spinosis – spiny
sylvatica – forest
vulgaris – common

As science evolves, some plants are reclassified (but not too often), which can be slightly confusing. For example, *Dicentra spectabilis* (Bleeding Heart) has recently been changed to *Lamprocapnos spectabilis*, placing it into a different genus.

The easiest way to get the hang of botanical names is to read the labels and observe the plants as they grow. Sometimes, you'll find that the name just sticks. If it doesn't, the plant won't stop growing in protest, so there's really nothing to stop you gardening! Growing plants can often be much easier than actually remembering or pronouncing the names, so let's carpe diem and grow a garden.

Gardening Terms Explained

Understanding terms as you are learning to garden can make things a lot easier, but there's no need to feel daunted, as many are self-explanatory. They are really all about knowing what to do with the plants – and that's what this book is going to help you with. Apart from some of the more complex scientific words and phrases, most terms will be easy to understand, especially for the home gardener who wants to create a low-maintenance, thriving garden.

Here are some common terms you will see on plant labels, books and instructions, to help you get the best out of your plants and garden:

SOIL AND COMPOST

Acidic – the pH of soil that is above neutral to acid. Some plants that thrive in acidic soil include pieris, rhododendron and blueberries.

Aeration – allowing air to get to the soil. Often used on lawns, where holes are made for air to reduce compaction of soil.

Alkaline – the majority of garden soil is alkaline. The majority of plants will grow in this.

Compost – decomposed living material that is soil-like and full of nutrients.

Humus – the organic matter in soil that provides nutrients and provides the soil with the ability to retain moisture.

Mulch – material such as bark or compost, used to retain moisture in the soil, smother weeds and protect plant roots.

Peat free – compost that has not had peat added to it for environmental reasons.

Perlite – volcanic glass that has been heat-treated and is used in potting soils to aid water retention.

Soil conditioner – material added to improve existing soil nutrients, structure and drainage.

Tilth – the health of soil. Good soil with a balance of water, air and nutrients is described as 'good tilth'.

Top dressing – spreading a new layer of soil on top of existing soil to provide more nutrients. It is often used in lawn care.

Topsoil – the precious upper layer of soil. Landscapers often refer to it as a perfectly consistent texture. It does not add nutrients but in agriculture it is essential for food growing.

Vermiculite – this is a mineral mixed into soil to help aerate it. Seeds can also be sown directly into it.

Well drained/good drainage – for plants that won't thrive in wet, waterlogged soil.

Well-rotted organic matter – decomposed organic materials that have not been subject to anything inorganic, such as homemade organic compost.

PLANTS

Annual – a plant that grows, flowers and seeds all in one season. It will not grow again and may not be an annual in warmer climates.

Bare root – a plant sold without soil around the roots and usually planted during November to March.

Bedding plants – used to make a temporary display and usually annual plants.

Biennial – growth begins in the first year and finishes in the second year, when it flowers and seeds.

Deciduous – trees and shrubs that drop their leaves over winter.

Doubles – flowers that have extra petals, or flowers within flowers.

Drought tolerant – plants that will grow in very dry conditions.

Epiphytes – plants that grow on another plant but cause no damage, such as many orchids.

Established – a plant that has settled into its home with a strong root system.

Evergreen – trees and shrubs that remain in leaf all year round.

Filler – plants used to fill the middle of a container that complement the other plants around them.

Half hardy – plants that will survive the cold but not a heavy frost.

Hardy – plants that will live through the cold winter period.

Herbaceous perennial – plants that die down over winter to the ground and grow again the following spring.

Perennial – plants that will grow again every spring. Some will grow for years and others just a few.

Self-seed – where the seeds have been produced and spread to the soil to grow.

Spiller – plants used at the edges of containers to trail or spill out of the pot.

Tender perennial – a plant that will grow year on year but will need winter protection from cold weather.

Thriller – plants in the centre or back of a container that add height and drama.

Volunteer – a plant that has self-seeded where it wants to, not where you've planted it.

SOWING AND GROWING

Bolting – where the plant flowers and sets seed too quickly. This often happens when plants are stressed (too hot/not enough water).

Dappled shade – similar to partial shade but often found in woodland or if plants are under deciduous trees.

Dead heading – removing faded flower or seed heads from a plant.

Deep shade – generally no sun at all.

Direct sow – seeds sown in the place you would like them to grow and mature.

Divide/split – a method of plant propagation where the plant is split into two through the roots, allowing more room for developing roots and creating another plant for growing.

Dormancy – the time of year when the plant is storing energy below the soil for growth when the weather warms up.

Full shade – less than four hours of sun per day.

Full sun – six or more hours of full sun a day.

Germination – when the seed starts to sprout and you can jump for joy.

Harden off – when a plant is gradually acclimatized to cooler temperatures before planting out permanently.

Microclimate – an area in a garden with a different climate from the general environment around it.

No dig – a method of gardening where the soil structure is retained by not digging it at all.

Overwintering – plants that grow over winter inside or outside. For example, autumn-planted onions are overwintered for harvests in spring. Some plants may need to be brought under cover to be overwintered, if they are tender.

Part sun/part shade – in direct sun for four to six hours per day.

Pinch out – removing some of the plant, mostly the tip or shoots, which encourages bushy plants to grow. Can be done by hand-pinching off the new growth at the tip.

Plug plant – germinated seedlings grown in a small cell with good root development.

Pruning – shaping, improving structure and growth of a plant. Mostly for trees, shrubs and perennials.

Root bound – when a plant's roots have filled out the root ball and have nowhere else to go.

Scorch – if a plant has yellow/brown leaves due to too much sun or pesticide use.

Seedling – the very young plant grown from seed.

Sheltered – planting in a position away from strong winds and nasty weather conditions.

Sow thinly – ensuring there aren't lots of seeds all sown together.

Succession sowing – sowing seeds every two to three weeks to ensure a constant harvest for as long as possible.

Thinning out – a method of removing weaker seedlings, allowing more room for the remaining ones to grow.

Transplanting – moving a plant from one growing medium to another.

Variegated – where any part of the plant has different colours. For example, the foliage might have two or three different stripes/patches caused by cell mutation.

NUTRIENTS AND CHEMICALS

Fungicide – a type of pesticide that kills fungal disease.

Herbicide – a type of pesticide that kills plants and often other wildlife.

NPK (nitrogen, phosphorus and potassium) – the three nutrients plants generally need to grow.

Organic – all-natural, sustainable and environmentally friendly gardening, without the use of chemicals.

Pesticide – chemicals targeted to kill certain pests.

Veganic – organic gardening without the use of any animal products.

Why Garden?

I am often asked why I love plants and that question always baffles me. My immediate thought is to wonder why anyone needs to ask that question! We simply cannot eat, drink or breathe without plants. Besides, flowers make such a difference to our mood. Just a few minutes in the garden, taking a moment out of a busy schedule, is enough to soothe the soul, and a garden can be both a happy space and a wildlife haven. We also have a responsibility to be caretakers of the planet, ensuring our impact is a positive one, and we can do that in small ways in our very own garden, immersing ourselves in the world of plants – even if we only have a little time to spare (see page 70).

We often see images in the media of big gardens, with huge, perfectly manicured lawns and well-tended hedges, and while that is one style of gardening, it doesn't reflect the reality of gardening for many. Smaller gardens, patios, balconies, windowsills and even houseplants are all ways to be in touch with the natural world and learn about the incredible attributes of plants.

A garden of any size can be whatever you want it to be, even if you are a busy bee. You might want a garden to grow your own food or to make your home look aesthetically softer, for example. Whatever your reason, the most important thing to reinforce is that gardening holistically without expectation is such a special activity. Taking inspiration from gorgeous landscape designs is a lovely way to implement snippets of ideas into your own garden, but if perfect borders are not your thing, that's fine too. Your garden is yours, for you to enjoy, so you should go about it however and whenever you

THE GARDEN GYM

Physically, gardening can be any level of exercise you choose on any given day. You will be improving dexterity, balance and strength at the same time as being surrounded by soothing greenery.

For a full cardio workout and to get your heart rate pumping, try some of these tasks:

- Digging, raking and forking
- Lifting and moving
- Pushing the wheelbarrow
- Pulling up deep-rooted weeds
- Clearing ground
- Cutting back trees and bushes
- Mowing the lawn.

For a gentle move and stretch, try the following:

- Light weeding
- Potting and repotting
- Harvesting
- Sowing seeds
- Transplanting
- Pruning plants
- Dead heading.

can, with the knowledge that you are helping yourself and the environment, no matter how much or how little time you have. Gardening has benefits for your health and wellbeing, the environment and also the wider community[3].

Wellbeing

Gardening really shines when it comes to looking after your mental health and wellbeing. Recent research[3] has shown that the more you garden, the greater the health benefits. Those who spend time gardening between two to three times a week have significantly improved wellbeing compared to those who don't garden at all. Plus, the more biodiverse your garden is, the greater the benefit.

REASONS TO BE CHEERFUL

There are many valuable reasons to get out in the garden and here are just some of the benefits:

- Simply being outside in the fresh air, absorbing vitamin D from the sunlight.
- Increasing serotonin levels (the happy hormone).
- Lowering blood pressure.
- Improving your outlook so that you feel calmer.
- Focusing on each gardening task in detail eases negative thoughts and boosts your self-esteem.
- Allowing yourself to take one task at a time and enjoy the moment improves concentration, which can then be applied to other areas in life.
- Nurturing plants brings hope, enlightenment and satisfaction.
- Enjoying a sense of pride in planting up a pretty container or a colourful hanging basket.
- Reconnecting with nature and bringing more wildlife into your surroundings.

Environment

The big, beautiful planet that we live on gives
life to every single organism on this earth, from
humans and animals to fish, bacteria, fungi
and, of course, trees and plants. We can make
a difference on this big ball of biodiversity we
live on through gardening. You may not feel
that you are changing the world but you
are. Gardening allows you to improve the
environment for the all-important bees,
butterflies, birds and insects that live around you.

THE GREEN GARDENER

Planting with sustainability and the environment in mind can
lead to a better understanding of the intricate connection we
have with nature, make a difference in combatting climate change
and leave a legacy for the future – even if it's simply through
maintaining pots on a balcony. Here are just some of the ways
that you can benefit the environment:

- Encourage pollinators by planting flowers.
- Grow shrubs with berries to feed birds over the winter.
- Build homes for bugs and hedgehogs.
- Choose recycled or upcycled and sustainable materials for
  landscaping, from pathways and seating to pots and planters.
- Collect rainwater for watering.
- Harvest seeds.
- Plant trees appropriate to your gardening space.
- Compost (see page 218).
- Grow your own food.
- Avoid synthetic fertilizers, pesticides and anything unnatural
  – this will help towards better air and soil quality.

FOR THE COMMON GOOD

Green spaces, especially those in urban areas, can be of particular benefit to the community. They can:

- Provide educational workshops and fun events.
- Be a source of fresh produce.
- Prevent loneliness by providing opportunities for teamwork, sharing, forming new social connections and a support system.
- Reduce negative impacts on the environment.
- Promote sustainable gardening.
- Provide homes for wildlife.
- Reduce flooding (by providing a natural break in concrete and paving).
- Improve the look and vibe of a city or neighbourhood.

Community

Getting your hands dirty and learning about plants can bring family, friends and communities together. Not everyone has a garden or space to grow and, even if they do, meeting people at a community garden to learn techniques can help with social inclusion and loneliness. So, if you are unsure where to start or you don't have any space of your own, check out a local community garden.

Of course, you can garden alone for time out and peace, or choose to involve family and friends – I like a mixture of the two. Days spent alone on the allotment are a precious haven of me-time, but inviting friends to help out is just as important. Meeting friends for dinner and giving them a bag of freshly harvested fruit and vegetables or a small handtied bouquet of cut flowers from the garden are such fulfilling gestures. I actually met and made a best friend by gifting a bunch of herbs. Opening up your world of gardening to others is empowering.

TOP TEN
PLANTS FOR WILDLIFE

Sharing your space with wildlife can be one of the most satisfying aspects of gardening. Seeing bees buzzing around or signs of toads and newts in a pond are enough to make anyone smile. A biodiverse garden is not only a haven for some of our most loved insects such as ladybirds, birds and butterflies, but it is also vital for shield bugs, lacewings and moths. A garden full of plants that are beneficial for wildlife also means a natural pest-control cycle will be in place, as ladybirds will feast on black fly, and hedgehogs will eat your slugs.

Here are my top ten plants for encouraging wildlife into your garden:

1. English ivy (*Hedera helix*)

- Great for bees, wasps, butterflies, birds, caterpillars and moths.
- Rich in nectar and pollen.
- Likes shade or sun, easy to grow, evergreen.
- Climbing habit, great for privacy.
- Prune early- to mid-spring and if needed again in early autumn.

2. Purple top (*Verbena bonariensis*)

- Attracts bees, butterflies and other pollinating insects.
- Tall, thin stems with bright purple flowers.
- Likes full sun and well-drained soil.
- Rich in nectar, pollen and seeds for birds.
- Will self-seed freely.

3. Stonecrop (*Sedum spectabile*)

- Great for honeybees and young queen bees.
- Adds interest in late summer/early autumn.
- Star-shaped pink flowers with fleshy leaves.
- Easy to grow, well-drained soil in full sun.
- You may see this reclassified as Hylotelephium.

4. Sweet box (*Sarcococca*)

- Has an incredible scent.
- Great for wildlife all year round.
- Evergreen glossy foliage.
- Creamy white flowers in winter, berries in summer.
- Loves to be grown in shade or sun, if the soil is moist.

5. Strawberry tree (*Arbutus unedo*)

- Evergreen tree, perfect for small gardens.
- Flowers and fruits at the same time.
- The 'strawberry' fruits are loved by birds.
- Plant in a sheltered spot in full sun.
- Grows up to 8m (26ft) in height.

6. Firethorn (*Pyracantha*)

- Good for boundary hedging or climbing up a wall.
- Thorny stems, you'll need some gloves.
- Packed full of berries for birds in autumn and winter.
- Can be shaped formally or left natural.
- Fragrant flowers in spring.

7. Teasel (*Dipsacus fullonum*)

- Stunning plant, attracts bees and birds, especially goldfinches.
- Biennial, so will flower in its second year.
- Sow directly where you want it to grow.
- Prefers moist soil.
- Grows up to 2m (6½ft) tall

8. Borage (*Borago officinalis*)

- Hardy flowering herb that bees love.
- Flowers from summer all the way through to autumn.
- Grows bushy and up to 60cm (24in) tall.
- Self-seeds freely.
- Likes sun and well-drained soil.

9. Globe thistle
(*Echinops bannaticus*)

- Spiky globe-shaped flowers on tall silvery stems.
- Loved by pollinators.
- Likes well-drained soil in full sun or part shade.
- Drought tolerant when established, water in extended dry periods.
- Looks great in a cottage-style border.

10. Guelder rose
(*Viburnum opulus*)

- Great as a wildlife hedge.
- Fragrant white flowers in summer.
- Foliage turns red and has berries in autumn.
- Plant in full sun or part shade.
- Grows to 5m (16ft) tall at a rate of 20–40cm (8–16in) per year.

CHAPTER 2

Understanding Your Space

Whether you are looking at a blank garden space and wondering where to start or your garden is established but you want to make some changes (however big or small your space is), this chapter explores the key aspects that you need to know to ensure you create a thriving garden. It can be very easy to look at your space, briefly see the sun and therefore think it is a sunny garden, when this may not be entirely the case. You'll discover why it is so important to know all of the areas of your garden, in sun or shade, so that you can choose the right plants for the right place, minimizing disappointment when plants don't grow and the cost of replacements.

Before you get planting, one of the most crucial parts of your garden to get to grips with is definitely your soil. Good soil is what plants need to grow. It's all too easy to buy plants, pop them in the garden

and wonder why they don't grow. Getting down and dirty in the soil is the first place to start. This chapter will explain different soil types, why pH levels are important, different types of compost and how soil really can save the world.

As you start getting your hands dirty, try to take some time to consider what you want from your space and how much time you will have to maintain your garden. In this chapter, you will find food for thought for a party garden, a chill-out area or a space for family fun. For those of you who have only a little time to get outside, you can choose from tasks that take ten minutes to those that will take longer, so you can prioritize what to do each time you're in the garden.

In this book, there is an emphasis on smaller spaces, balcony gardens, patios and using vertical spaces, because we don't all have large gardens. In the following pages, you will find lots of hints and tips for how to maximize and care for a small space – from dwarf trees for containers to vertical gardening options.

Where to Start

It can be daunting wondering where to start if you are thinking of shaking up your garden for the first time. Even wondering what to plant in containers can seem a bewildering task. No matter what size of area you are working with, a large border or a balcony trough, there are some easy tips looking at factors such as size, aspect, sun and shade to get you started. These will help you to choose that all-important right plant for the right place.

NO WRONG WAY

Despite the theory, often plants do thrive in places you would least expect. So, if you have a shady spot but you are desperate for a plant that prefers full sun, then plant it anyway and see how well it grows. One of the great joys of gardening is experimentation.

OBSERVE AND VISUALIZE

For long-lasting, thriving and sustainable gardening, it is a good idea to get to know your garden well. On a first glance out of the window, you might think an area that you want to plant is in full sun, but do you see it at every hour of the day? Is it ever shaded by a tree, structure or building as the sun moves in the sky? Remember that full sun means more than six hours per day and that no part of the plant is shaded. I have a balcony that I was told was in full sun but the railings shade most of the plants, meaning that at various points throughout the day different pots are subject to a part sun/part shade aspect. So, in fact, the balcony is in part sun/part shade. This gives me a better idea of what will thrive and allows me to place each pot according to whether they prefer morning sun or the very hot afternoon sun.

I would always recommend observing your space. Be curious about everything you can see. Think about what is already thriving (or not) and also what wildlife you are sharing your garden with. Consider what is growing in your neighbours' gardens, because this gives a good clue as to what type of soil and aspect you have – so take a peek over the fence.

Next, visualize what you would like your garden to look like. What colours do you want? Would you prefer a cool, calm feeling with white, lilac and lots of green, or a splash of pizazz with hot colours such as yellow, orange and red? Are there birds nesting in your trees and do you want to attract a certain species? Build the picture in your mind, sketch your ideas on paper or just write a list. All of this will help you to get started and build on your plan (see more about this on page 52).

SIZE MATTERS

Whatever space you are growing in, size does matter. You'll need to know how big your planting area is to ensure you choose the correct-sized plants. The mature size of the plant is what matters, so when you buy a plant in a pot, remember to consider its ultimate height and width of growth and make sure there will be enough space around it. If you are planting containers on a patio or balcony, you'll need to decide if you will have lots of small pots or just a few big pots. Each option will provide an entirely different look and feel. Plus, if you want to grow a plant that requires a lot of root space, you'll need a bigger pot.

PREPARE A PLAN

1. Whether you're undertaking a full garden redesign or planting a small border, grab your measuring tape and measure it up. Then sketch out a plan. It doesn't have to be a piece of art, it's just a reference for you to work with. If you want it to be more detailed, you could also draw it to scale.
2. Measure and record the overall size of your garden space.
3. Sketch it roughly on paper, or choose an appropriately sized sheet of paper to represent your garden space.
4. Add in the rough dimensions of permanent structures such as sheds and greenhouses.
5. Add the position of water and/or an electricity supply.
6. Include patios, pathways, benches and anything else notable.
7. Measure and draw up your borders or new borders, perhaps including where you will put pots or hanging baskets.
8. Don't forget to measure vertical structures too – making use of all space is ideal. You can grow climbers up fences, create a green wall or install arches for vines.

MEASURING WITH SAND

If you need to measure out a new border, sprinkle sand on the ground to mark out the area, then step back to check it is where you want it to be before you dig (if on a lawn) or smash up (if on concrete). You can keep amending the border edge with sand until you are happy with the size and shape. Sand is also a useful tool for marking out where pots will stand on a patio or balcony. Just sprinkle a circle the size of a pot and see how you feel about it. This method is particularly useful for large, ceramic pots that will be heavy to move after planting up.

ASPECT

Knowing your aspect is key to a thriving garden resulting in little waste (including money and time). Whimsical purchases from the plant nursery are fully justified, but ultimately a garden will come together better if you plant your purchases where they will have the most chance of flourishing.

Step 1: Find Your Direction

The way your garden faces will determine how much sun your plants will or won't bask in during the day. Using a compass (there is usually one available on a mobile phone), stand outside the back of your house or on your balcony to figure out which way is south and therefore the aspect of your garden.

North – will get the least light of all aspects and can also be damp.

East – will get mostly morning light as the sun rises.

South – will be in the most sunlight for the day.

West – will have mostly afternoon and evening light.

Step 2: Check for Shade

When you know the aspect, look at which areas are shaded by trees, buildings or other structures as the sun moves during the day. A south-facing garden with a huge tree will mean that some areas will be in part or dappled shade.

MICROCLIMATES – THE EXCEPTION

Microclimates are areas within a garden that are different to the rest of the space. They may be damper or drier, perhaps warmer or colder. An example might be a zone that is lower than most of the garden, which collects water or freezes more easily. It could be the one spot in the garden that is always shaded, even though the rest is in full sun. In fact, a whole garden can be a microclimate in itself. Even exotic gardens can be created in cooler climates if trees, water and light are used to enhance the temperature and humidity. Microclimates can be big or small, and, if you work with the elements rather than against them, these zones can provide you with an opportunity to grow plants entirely different to anywhere else in the garden. A damp corner where bog plants will grow, or a dry patch alongside a wall where drought-tolerant plants can grow, are areas where you can get creative.

Step 3: Record the Sunlight

To see how the sunlight moves across your space throughout the day, draw the outline of your garden onto a piece of paper. On a sunny day, look outside every hour to see where the sunlight is falling at that moment. Draw a line to represent this on your garden outline.

BUDGET

It is easy to spend a lot of money on a garden but it can also be easy and rewarding to do it on a tight budget. Whichever way you decide to go, setting a budget will stop you from running away with yourself when online shopping or buying plants on a whim – although I am guilty of both!

Write a list of what is most important to do first. Is it hard landscaping, buying pots and containers, compost and accessories, or is it all about getting the plants in the ground? When you know where you want to start, make sure it all fits in your budget.

Gardening easily and cheaply doesn't have to be difficult at all. You'll notice, unsurprisingly, that creating a vibrant space on a budget is far more environmentally friendly than spending a packet.

Shop around: from materials to plants, there are many places to purchase from (see page 111), so make sure you look at a few different places before buying, in order to bag yourself a bargain.

Don't be shy: if a friend or family member has a plant that would sit pretty in your garden, then ask for a cutting, to save some seeds or to divide the plant so that you can have a share. Even a neighbour might be willing to help out.

Recycle and upcycle: pallets can be made into chairs, compost bins and tables; old tyres, wooden crates and bins make great planters;

a butler sink can be renovated to make a small wildlife pond; a wooden stepladder will make a great plant stand; you can even plant in old tea cups, boots and drawers.

Ask for help: if you are tackling a particularly tricky task, why not ask a friend or family member to help you out? Make a day of it and have lunch in the garden as well.

Swap plants: find a local plant or seed swap and see what you can find. Many gardeners have excess seeds or cuttings they will happily gift to a newbie.

Bare roots: planting bare roots over winter is much cheaper than buying the plants when they are potted and in flower. The plant will arrive looking – quite frankly – dead, but it's not! It will be in dormancy, storing its energy for growth in spring.

Grow from seed: sowing seeds and later saving seeds for the following year is the best way to watch a plant grow. As you nurture it through to flourishing, the whole process is magical – and cheaper than buying fully grown plants.

Source free stuff: often tree surgeons need to dispose of wood chip, which they will often deliver for free. It's a great material with many uses, especially for pathways. Check out local forums online, where people often offer their discards for free, such as compost, paving slabs or old benches.

Collect rainwater: get a barrel or water butt, ensure nothing can fall in (such as fledgling birds and other wildlife) and allow nature to fill it up. Use this to water your plants and save on your bill. Some councils give water butts away for free during environmental campaign times, as will some water companies.

Get to Know Your Soil

When we admire gardens, we are usually looking at the colourful flowers, the statuesque trees or the butterflies gracing the sky. We might also comment on a new furniture set, the manicured lawn or stunning wildflowers. But do we ever look at the soil? Generally, we want to cover it up with plants – no one admires bare patches. However, in the case of soil, it's what's beneath the surface that counts; where the roots draw up the water and nutrients, there is a whole other world, literally supporting life on Earth.

Soil Saves the World!

To fully appreciate the importance of soil for a healthy garden, you need to learn about its essential role in sustaining life as we know it. This will give you a completely different perspective when you next put your garden fork in the ground beneath you.

Soil is full of life. In just one teaspoon of soil there are billions of living organisms and together, they work in an incredible, complex and intricate system, building the foundation to the earth we walk on. From nematodes to earthworms, protozoa and bacteria, they are all busily working away along with mycorrhizae fungi and much more. Mycorrhizae fungi helps plant roots to absorb nutrients from the soil and can be bought to add to compost when you plant out new plants.

Then there is the cheerful *Mycobacterium vaccae*, a naturally occurring bacteria found in soil, which has been shown to make people happy! It triggers the release of serotonin and may even improve your brain function[1].

Healthy soil is one component that is essential to our survival. Others are sunlight, air and water. If soil is depleted of the incredible life within it, it becomes dirt which is no good for anyone or anything. Soil is also the largest source of organic carbon, holding approximately 75 per cent of land carbon, which in turn keeps it out of the atmosphere. Soil, therefore, is crucial in helping to mitigate climate change. So, when you cultivate healthy, organic soil, you are helping to save the world.

In the home garden, getting to know your soil is as important as choosing your plants. There are a few factors to consider when cultivating soil, then you will soon be on your way to a beautiful garden.

SOIL PH

Depending on your location, your soil can be vastly different to another area of the country or, in fact, a different area down your road. At times, soil can vary even within your own garden. Use a soil test kit to take samples from different areas in your garden to see what pH level you have. Test kits are available online and in plant nurseries, and are very cheap and easy to use.

There are also a couple of other, natural indicators of your soil pH level. The majority of plants grow well in neutral-to-alkaline soil conditions, but there are some plants that thrive in acidic soil. Camellia, willow and magnolia tend to like slightly acidic conditions, and flourishing rhododendrons, azalea and blueberries are a sure sign that your soil is on the acidic side. So, if your neighbours or your local area have many of these plants, take note.

Another natural indictator is the colour of big-leaf hydrangeas. Hydrangea flowers can be blue or pink depending on the aluminium in the soil, which is drawn up through the roots. This is possible in acidic soil but not in alkaline soils. So if your hydrangea stays pink, you have an alkaline soil; if it grows blue each year, then you have acidic soil. A white hydrangea will always be white.

By using ericaceous compost, you can alter the soil towards a lower pH (lower = acidic) in order to grow plants that prefer acidic soil, but this will take maintenance. Soil, like everything else in the natural world, prefers to be in its natural state.

TYPE OF SOIL

Getting in contact with the soil is the best way to start identifying what soil type you have. Of course, if your soil is used by pets or wildlife, or you have any cuts on your hands, then gloves will be preferable! In your hand, mix a handful of soil with a bit of water. As you roll the wet soil, feel the texture between your fingers and see which characteristics you can identify from the list below:

Loam is what every gardener wants – it's the perfect mix for plants. It will roll into a ball but it won't be sticky like clay.

Clay soil is sticky, smooth and will roll easily into a ball.

Sandy soil drains well but can dry out quickly. Rolled in your hands, the soil will crumble away with ease.

Peat is acidic but not so often found in gardens. It is dark and spongy when you squeeze it in your hands.

Chalk soil is alkaline and will have a white, stony chalkiness when you collect some.

Once you have identified your soil type, make sure to read plant instructions (see page 106) to check which plants prefer your soil type, and choose accordingly.

Moist or Dry?

Of course, when you water your garden as needed, the soil will be moist, but there will also be areas in your garden that are more dry or moist depending on their position, meaning that more or less water is needed. If you plant specifically with this in mind, it can save you a lot of time in maintaining your plants!

Dry soil/sunny: this is the perfect area for drought-tolerant plants. Try a Mediterranean-style garden with Russian sage (*Perovskia*), yarrow (*Achillea*), African lily (*Agapanthus*), Lavender (*Lavandula*) and an olive tree (*Olea europaea*).

Dry soil/shady: often this area will be under trees, making the conditions cool just like in a woodland area. Grow wood fern (*Dryopteris*), holly-leaved barberry (*Mahonia*), windflowers (*Anemone*), Christmas rose (*Helleborus niger*), sow bread (*Cyclamen*) and lily of the valley (*Convallaria majalis*).

Moist soil/sunny: this is perfect for a bog garden. Most plants that like to keep their feet wet will grow well in these conditions. Try arum lily (*Zantedeschia*), leopard plant (*Ligularia*), yellow flag (*Iris pseudacorus*), purple loosestrife (*Lythrum salicaria*) and Candelabra primulas.

Moist soil/shady: this will be a cool spot, unlike a bog garden. Grow plants such as plantain lily (*Hosta*), snake's head fritillary (*Fritillaria meleagris*), common bistort (*Persicaria bistorta*), common meadow rue (*Thalictrum*) and false goat's beard (*Astilbe*).

UNDERSTANDING DIFFERENT COMPOSTS

There are various different composts to use – if in doubt, use a peat-free multipurpose compost (digging up bogs for peat is detrimental to the climate). Here's a handy list of the compost you can look out for:

Seed compost is a fine compost made for seed sowing. Seeds don't need nutrients to germinate so it is a light mix with low nutrients.

Potting compost is a mixture of materials, resulting in a light compost that is good for pots and hanging baskets.

Multipurpose (no peat) is an all-rounder. Some will be better than others; many will have the addition of a slow-release fertilizer mixed in.

Ericaceous compost is specifically for plants that don't thrive in alkaline soils and prefer a lower pH towards the acidic range.

Mushroom compost is a rich organic mix, often made with a variety of materials, from hay and straw to corn and horse manure.

Plant-based compost is made entirely with plants and has become available on the market more recently. This is what I use for all of my growing needs.

Houseplant compost is light and well drained, often with the addition of grit or sand for extra drainage. Multipurpose compost can be used for houseplants, but it does tend to encourage fungus gnats.

Coir is made from the fibrous material in between the outer husk and the coconut. It holds moisture well and expands in water, and is often used to bulk out compost rather than on its own. It is also used for seed sowing.

Speciality compost (for cacti/orchids/succulents, for example) have a variety of materials and uses for specific plants. They are worth a try but not necessary, in my experience.

TOP TEN
SHADE-FRIENDLY PLANTS

If you have a shady area in your garden, it's a common misconception to think you can't make it look good. In fact, in my old cottage garden, the area planted up with shade-loving perennials was my favourite part of the garden. There are so many plants that thrive in shade, and it can be exciting to fill a border and see it come to life, even though the sun isn't shining on it. It feels like you are cheating the elements but, of course, that's not true at all. By choosing the correct plants for the area, you are working together with nature and turning an otherwise empty space into a riot of colour, foliage and texture.

Here are my top ten plants for brightening up a shady patch:

1. Coral bells (*Heuchera*)

- Variety of brightly coloured foliage.
- Tall flower spikes.
- Likes well-drained, moist soil.
- Likes dappled shade.
- Easy to grow in pots.

2. Epimediums, also known as fairy wings (*Epimedium*)

- Variety of colours – yellow, red, white and lilac.
- Pretty little flowers.
- Use leaf mulch to keep them happy.
- Likes dappled to deep shade.
- Easy to grow under a tree.

3. Hardy geraniums, also known as cranesbills (*Geranium*)

- Variety of colours from pink and violet to white.
- Great ground cover.
- Sun or shade (check the label).
- Needs water to establish and in dry weather.
- Very little care needed.

4. Foxgloves (*Digitalis*)

- Colours from pink and peach to white.
- Bell-shaped flowers loved by bees.
- Biennial or perennial (check the label).
- Likes moist, well-drained soil.
- Easy to care for in shade.

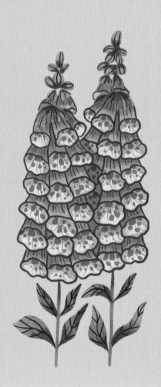

5. Hostas, also known as plantain lily (*Hosta*)

- Variety of exquisite foliage from variegated to crinkled green, silver and blue.
- Some flowers have a scent.
- Grows well in pots (will need more water).
- Insects use the large leaves for shade.
- Light shade preferable.

6. Astilbes, also known as false goat's beard (*Astilbe*)

- Fluffy flowers that look like candy floss.
- Various shades of pink and white.
- Likes moist, well-drained soil.
- Good bog plants.
- Easy perennial to grow in part shade.

7. Pulmonarias, also known as lungwort (*Pulmonaria*)

- Blooms in early spring with purple, pink, white and bluish flowers.
- Green foliage has white/silver spots.
- Likes moist, well-drained soil.
- Great ground-cover perennial.
- Happy in full shade.

8. Aquilegia, also known as granny's bonnet (*Aquilegia*)

- Variety of colours from yellow to pink.
- Likes moist, well-drained soil.
- Most are happy in sun or part shade.
- Will self-seed freely.
- Easy care, very little water needed after established.

9. Himalayan blue poppy (*Meconopsis betonicifolia*)

- One of the most gorgeous 'blue' flowers you'll find.
- A tricky one to grow, but so worth it.
- Do not let them dry out in summer.
- Likes cool, damp conditions in part shade.
- Likes moist, rich, well-drained soil.

10. Astrantia, also known as greater masterwort (*Astrantia major*)

- Small pretty flower clusters surrounded by colourful bracts.
- Many colours from red and deep purple to white and pink.
- Likes moist, part shade (will grow in dryer conditions).
- Herbaceous perennial that will keep coming back.
- Easy to care for in a shade border.

How Do You Want to Use Your Space?

When you have decided how much time you will be able to spend tending to your garden, take some time to consider how you will use it. Think about what you want from your space – not just what it will look like, but how you want to use it, who will be enjoying it – for example, do you want it to be a vegetable garden, an ornamental garden or a mixture of both?

RELAXING SPACE

If you want your garden to be a place of peacefulness and calm, where you can sit and read, practise yoga or meditate, think about creating privacy with trees and installing a water feature for tranquility. Have an area where you can sit quietly. If you have space, make sure there is some even, soft ground where you can exercise.

Water features don't need to be grand – a small fountain, bird bath or shallow reflection pool of any size will provide a focal point and somewhere to sit near to relax. Pick up a concrete or ceramic pot from an antiques yard, add some plants, including a water lily, and take time to feel at peace. (See page 93 for more details on bucket ponds).

Depending on your aspect, choose plants that encourage peacefulness and provide a calming sensory experience when you sit in the garden. Think about what colours might help you to unwind. In a serene garden, the plants tend to be white, blue, pink and purple with lots of green foliage. Fragrance is important, so include plants such as honeysuckle (*Lonicera*), lavender (*Lavandula*), gardenia (*Gardenia*), roses (*Rosa*) and lilac (*Syringa*) around the areas where you will walk or sit, where possible. These will help to provide those relaxing vibes.

Other plants that will help create a tranquil space include:

Bamboo gives a beautiful, peaceful feel and as it can grow quickly, a young plant will soon grow enough to make you feel relaxed in your safe space. Try black bamboo (*Phyllostachys nigra*) for something different; although a little slower growing than other bamboos, the stems are black and the foliage is bright green. I would recommend growing bamboo in a container, so that its roots cannot go wild in your garden, and placing it in a cosy corner.

Japanese maples (*Acer*) and dogwood (*Cornus kousa*) provide a wonderful sense of tranquility and peacefulness. Both can be grown in containers or in the ground and will provide you with wonderful colours, flowers and berries.

PARTY TIME

If your garden is going to be all about fun, it's time to start thinking about lights, zesty colours and maybe even a pizza oven! Add a touch of your personality to the garden with quirky accessories and plenty of areas for entertaining your friends and family.

Al fresco dining – create a patio area with a long table and benches to host family and friends for food and drinks. Whether your taste is a modern or rustic table, you can adorn it with small vases of cut flowers to impress your friends. If you have enough room, include a pizza oven or BBQ nearby too.

Lights are essential for an outside party and can include anything from colourful fairy lights to netted lights that hang down a wall. Bistro lights are particularly popular and can be hung above the table or in the trees surrounding your entertaining space. All lights work well for a balcony space.

Brightly coloured plants will bring a sense of joy to your space. Try a mixture of red-hot poker (*Kniphofia*), desert lily (*Eremurus*), daylily (*Hemerocallis*), black-eyed Susan (*Rudbeckia*) and crocosmia (*Crocosmia*). The colours will look vibrant and add to an exciting atmosphere as you party into the night.

CHILD AND PET HAVEN

If your garden is going to be filled with football goal posts, swings and trampolines, the most important thing is to just enjoy it. However, there are some ways to minimize damage and keep the lawn looking as good as possible, including choosing tougher grass seed, plants that are harder to snap and unbreakable containers.

Safety check – it's a good idea to make sure that your plants aren't toxic to humans or pets. Ivy (*Hedera*), gladioli (*Gladiolus*), tulips (*Tulipa*), chrysanthemum (*Chrysanthemum*), oleander (*Nerium oleander*) and begonias (*Begonia*) are all toxic for dogs, for example. You could try planting anything toxic well out of the way – perhaps at the back of a border – but not planting them at all is the safest bet. Do your research and teach children and the family pets to stay away where necessary.

Child area – allocate one area of the garden for children to grow their own food and flowers. This could be a a corner, a small raised bed or in containers. Get your little ones involved in learning how the garden grows, where their food comes from and what it takes to nurture something. Great seeds for children to grow outside are nasturtiums (*Tropaeolum majus*), sugar snap peas (*Pisum sativum* 'Sugar Snap'), sunflowers (*Helianthus*) and microgreens, as they provide a quick crop.

Tough plants are less likely to be damaged by a football gone awry, so when you are planting your borders, research some sturdy plants that are almost football proof! Ornamental grasses and New Zealand flax (*Phormium*) are pretty tough, as are lady's mantle (*Alchemilla mollis*), Lenten rose (*Helleborus*) and the toughest of herbs, rosemary (*Salvia rosmarinus*).

How Much Time Do You Have for Gardening?

It's exciting when your adventure begins in the garden and you start putting your plans into action. If you're anything like me, before you've even thought about what you actually want to achieve, you will have already planted a few favourites from the garden centre! Before you go too far, consider the amount of time you will be able to spend in the garden maintaining it. Whether you are getting your hands dirty or just relaxing, your garden is meant to be a special place where you can connect with the natural world, nurture plants and feel relaxed. A garden with lots of work to do when you don't have time can be more stressful than relaxing, so thinking about how much time you'll have to keep it just how you want it is top priority.

The amount of time you will need to maintain your space will depend on whether your garden is a balcony or patio, has a large lawn or is just a windowsill, and also on how you want to keep it. Wild gardens are more low maintenance and can be wildlife havens, but formal, perfectly tended gardens can also be great for wildlife if the right plants are chosen, although they will require more time to keep them looking great.

TEN-MINUTE JOBS

- Water containers and the lawn, if required.
- Dead head plants and clear debris.
- Sweep the patio.
- Feed the birds.
- Cut flowers for a vase.

TEN MINUTES PER WEEK

If you are on a tight timescale but you would love some quick and easy colour, try planting containers full of annual bedding plants. Plant them with some peat-free multipurpose compost and water as needed. Keep dead heading them and they will flower on and on. Each season, shake things up with some changes so that you always have a fresh display perfect for the time of year. You can also create stunning containers with a mixture of perennials and annuals.

Thrillers, Spillers and Fillers

The three elements of a spectacular container are:

1. **Thriller** – a plant that makes a statement and draws your eye to it. It could be tall or especially vibrant.
2. **Spiller** – a plant that hangs over the edge.
3. **Filler** – the plants used to fill the spaces around the thriller and spiller.

For a brightly coloured, vibrant pot, try:

Thriller: Canna (*Canna* 'Durban') – tall, bright orange flowers with an almost psychedelic foliage.

Spiller: Million bells (*Calibrachoa* 'Yellow Chiffon') – lots of bright yellow flowers.

Filler: Coleus (*Solenostemon* 'Black Dragon') – velvety textured, dark foliage complementing the thriller and spiller.

For a pot full of frills, try:

Thriller: Snapdragon 'Bells Pink' (*Antirrhinum majus* 'Bells Pink') – short stems with a profusion of bright pink flowers.

Spiller: Lobelia 'Fountain White' (*Lobelia erinus* 'Fountain White') – trailing masses of small white flowers.

Filler: *Petunia* 'Surfinia Purple Heart' – white flowers with purple/pinkish hearts (these will spill over a little too).

For a funky, sensory pot, try:

Thriller: Woodland sage 'Caradonna' (*Salvia nemorosa* 'Caradonna') – tall, purple flower spikes.

Spiller: Nasturtium 'Princess of India' (*Tropaeolum majus* 'Princess of India') – vibrant red, edible flowers and dark, edible foliage.

Filler: Shining-white ragwort (*Senecio candidans* 'Angel Wings') – silvery/white leaves are velvety to touch.

Wildflower Pots

Pots of wildflowers are another easy way to grow pretty, colourful flowers and attract pollinators with little maintenance. Simply sow some wildflower seeds into your chosen container in September or May and water as required. The great thing about sowing a wildflower pot is that you never know exactly what will grow each season and year after year. Often, you'll have different flowers all spring and summer long, from ox-eye daisy (*Leucanthemum vulgare*) and red campion (*Silene dioica*) to cornflower (*Centaurea cyanus*), common poppy (*Papaver rhoeas*) and many more. Another option to try are 'seedballs', which are a mix of wildflower seeds already rolled into a ball – you simply throw the ball where you want the flowers to grow.

Annual Seeds

Growing any plant from seed is extremely satisfying, and for a quick turnaround with easy care, sowing annuals (a plant that grows, flowers and seeds all in one season) is a great way to fill garden space and attract pollinators. Annuals also make wonderful cut flowers, so can provide you with a supply of flowers in the home taken from outside your doorstep. As they are easy and quick to grow, you don't need much time at all to achieve good results.

TOP FIVE HARDY ANNUALS TO GROW

1. **Godetia** *(Clarkia amoena)* – pink and white frilly-edged petals on tall stems that flower on and on.
2. **Pot marigold** *(Calendula officinalis)* – bright orange and yellow flowers that bloom almost all year round.
3. **Love-in-a-mist** *(Nigella damascena)* – stunning seed heads and whimsical flowers, usually in blue, lilac and white.
4. **Bishop's weed** *(Ammi majus)* – an umbellifer (a plant in the parsley family that has its flowers arranged in umbels, or clusters) that looks a lot like cow parsley and grows all summer.
5. **Honeywort** *(Cerinthe major)* – silvery blue leaves and pollen-rich purple flowers.

TOP FIVE HALF-HARDY ANNUALS TO GROW

1. **Cosmea** *(Cosmos bipinnatus)* – a tall plant with feathery foliage and mostly pink, white, dark purple or yellow flowers.
2. **Flowering tobacco** *(Nicotiana alata)* – funnel-shaped, colourful flowers that come alive at night with a sweet fragrance.
3. **Zinnia** *(Zinnia elegans)* – colourful, daisy-like flowers in many colours.
4. **Spider flower** *(Cleome spinosa)* – architectural-looking, pink and white clusters of flowers; few are needed to fill a small space.
5. **Strawflower** *(Helichrysum bracteatum)* – everlasting flowers from pink to white and orange to purple that look incredible in dried-flower arrangements.

Annuals are either 'hardy' or 'half hardy' (see Gardening Terms Explained, page 33) and sowing depends on how eager you are at the beginning of the year! Hardy annuals can be sown in autumn then again in spring, which means the seeds sown in autumn will grow in time for early summer and the springs seeds will take you through a long summer of flowers into early autumn. Half-hardy annuals can be sown directly where you want them to grow but after the last frosts, as the soil needs to be warmed up after winter, so I tend to sow mine during early May. Don't forget, though, that frosts in May can catch you unawares, so always check the weather in your area and always read the seed packet instructions (see Seed Packet Descriptions, page 109, for further guidance).

There are two different methods for sowing annuals:

Direct sow – this is by far the easiest and quickest way of growing annual flowers.

1. The tiny seeds will struggle in heavy or clumpy soil, so fork in some well-rotted organic matter first of all to improve the drainage and help the roots to grow. Next, prepare the area where you want them to grow by raking the soil to a fine tilth.
2. Make a 1cm (½in) deep line with your hand trowel or rake. Always check the seed packet instructions for sowing depths, to be sure.
3. Water the soil (you do this before you sow the seeds so that the water doesn't wash them away).
4. Sprinkle your seeds about 5cm (2in) apart and cover over with soil.
5. Label your rows or mark them with sand, so that after the winter months you don't forget where you've sown!

Under cover – if you want to start your seeds off early in the spring before the soil warms up, they will need to be kept under cover somewhere, such as in a greenhouse, coldframe or on a windowsill. However, try to avoid sowing any seed too early in excitement, because they can struggle in low light and later sowings tend to be much stronger in the long term. I sow seeds under cover from early April. Some plants do not like to have their roots disturbed, so direct sowing is still preferable and much easier from May.

1. Sow seeds into pots of seed compost (any pots will do, including recycled food containers). (See Sowing and Growing, page 152.)
2. Keep moist and in a light position.

PROLONGING ANNUALS

Dead head annuals regularly to keep them flowering for as long as possible. If you allow some to self-seed, by leaving the flower heads after flowering to go to seed, you'll find them growing the following year in your garden. Or, collect the seeds on a dry day and store them in a cool, dry place over winter, ready for sowing again in the spring.

Bulb Lasagne

A bulb lasagne is a super-quick space-saving idea for impactful spring or summer flowering in one pot. The technique has earned its name due to the layering of bulbs in one pot. Spring-flowering bulbs should be planted in autumn, and summer-flowering bulbs planted in spring. This will result in two containers planted up for spring and summer flowering with barely any maintenance needed, just some dead heading. The number of bulbs you plant will depend on the size of pot you are using. I am all for packing them in for maximum effect – you can plant the bulbs close together but not touching.

1. Grab a deep container and some peat-free multipurpose compost.
2. Fill about one third of the pot with compost and gently firm down.
3. Plant a layer of bulbs, then cover with a layer of compost.
4. Plant a second layer of bulbs and cover with another layer of compost.
5. Plant a third layer of bulbs, and add another layer of compost.
6. Water, then add some winter-flowering bedding plants on top for interest over the colder months before your bulbs start to grow. Try pansies (*Viola*), sow bread (*Cyclamen*) and heathers (*Calluna*).

For a spring lasagne, try the following bulbs:

Bottom layer – tulips (*Tulipa*).

Middle layer – daffodils (*Narcissus*) and/or hyacinths (*Hyacinthus*).

Top layer – crocuses (Crocus) and/or grape hyacinths (*Muscari*).

For a summer lasagna, use the following bulbs:

Bottom layer – Asiatic lilies (*Lilium*) or pineapple lilies (*Eucomis*).

Middle layer – tiger flowers (*Tigridia*) and/or Bulgarian honey garlic (*Allium bulgaricum*).

Top layer – early bulbous irises (*Iris reticulata*) and/or freesias (*Freesia*).

LOW-MAINTENANCE FRUIT
AND VEGETABLES

The following five fruit and vegetables plants are easy plants to grow if you have an hour to spend in the garden each week.

Carrots

- Easy to grow, ideally in a sandy, light soil mix, or in a raised bed or container. (Growing carrots in a stony, lumpy or freshly manured soil tends to make the roots form in all manner of shapes, although wonky roots are still delicious, edible and fun!)
- Sow seeds at 1cm (½in) deep into a mixture of multipurpose compost and sand, cover over with a little compost and water in. If you sow every two weeks throughout the spring and summer, you'll have an abundance for many months.
- Thin out young seedlings (you can use them to make a tasty pesto), making plenty of room for each carrot to grow, and you'll be harvesting the best-flavoured carrots you've ever eaten in approximately 60 days.
- If you are growing carrots lower than 60cm (24in) off the ground, cover them with some mesh to stop root fly devouring them before you do.

Swiss chard

- Easy to grow in the ground, raised beds or in pots.
- Quite prolific and looks stunning in both an ornamental border or a vegetable patch.
- Rainbow chard has brightly coloured stems that range from pinkish-red to yellow.
- Full of nutrition – you can eat young leaves raw but as they grow bigger, add them to cooking just like spinach.
- Sow seeds from early spring to early autumn at about 1.5cm (¾in) deep in a sunny spot and water in well.

Onions

- Incredibly easy to grow from 'sets' (small onion bulbs specifically for growing into full-sized onions) and quick to harvest.
- Plant sets in full sun and well-drained soil, which has been prepared with some well-rotted manure, during spring or early autumn.
- Don't plant onions too deep – around 3cm (1¼in) is enough.
- Plant them out during September or October and they will soon grow the following spring. Alternatively, you can also plant sets in March or April.
- When you first plant, cover with netting to stop the birds pinching them.
- It can take three or more months before harvest but, in the meantime, there is very little you'll need to do to them.

Microgreens

- These edible seedlings will grow at any time of year – outside in the warmer months and inside a greenhouse, or even on a windowsill in the colder months.
- Seeds that you can sow as microgreens include kale, sprouts, rocket, mustard, basil, parsley, broccoli, radish, beetroot and peas.
- Sow seeds in a tray of compost, keep them moist and leave them in a bright place.
- Harvest them at up to 10cm (4in) tall, long before they mature. You'll be able to snip them in ten days to three weeks and add them into soups, smoothies and salads, or use as garnishes.
- They pack a punch of nutrition (vitamins and antioxidants) and flavour, even more so than the fully matured vegetable!

Strawberries

- One of the most satisfyingly sweet crops to grow at home, ideal for any size of space.
- Grow well in hanging baskets, pots and raised beds, as well as directly in the ground.
- Many varieties to choose from, including those that fruit at different times throughout the summer and almost bird-proof white strawberries (birds think they aren't ripe!).
- Plant 'runners' or young plants out in spring or autumn about 30cm (12in) apart in a peat-free compost or a prepared bed with some well-rotted organic matter. 'Runners' are stems that have nodes on with baby plants, which you can put in a pot of compost to grow more plants. If you don't want to grow more plants, you will still need to snip them off and tidy up the plants in order for them to continue thriving.
- Water as they establish and in dry weather, and keep the weeds away.

- Mow the lawn.
- Weed.
- Prune.
- Sow seeds.
- Mulch around plants.
- Harvest fruit and vegetables.

ONE HOUR PER WEEK

If you can grab an hour in the garden at some point during your week, you could grow more plants. Many don't require much maintenance apart from watering, dead heading and harvesting, as well as a little upkeep in spring and autumn. Growing herbs (see page 164) is an ideal way to attract pollinators, enjoy a variety of flowers and have a productive garden with low input. There are also many fruits and vegetables that don't need a huge amount of care and can be grown in small spaces and/or containers. When growing your own food, remember that you need to factor in time for harvesting and storing.

Perennial Borders

Perennial plants (those which grow again every spring) don't need as much care as you would expect when they are established. The main jobs required weekly would be to dead head, weed, cut some for a vase and generally tidy up. In dry weather, the plants may need regular watering depending on whether they are thirsty plants or not. Always keep an eye out for pests and diseases. Keeping a check at least weekly will help you really get to know your plants better.

UP TO HALF A DAY PER WEEK

If you have buckets of time on your hands to garden, the jobs will just keep on flowing. There is always something to do and often one job leads to another! But before you know it, the garden will be shipshape and you will be ready to start a new project – move some plants or create a new bed. Once you have the gardening bug, it really never stops.

FOUR-HOUR JOBS (Including all of the above):

- Edge the lawn, if formal.
- Thin out seedlings and pot on (see page 156).
- Thorough weeding.
- Clean pots, seed trays and tools.
- Feed plants (see page 186).

HOW TO GROW A LAWN

In the traditional sense, a lawn is a square of green, perfectly manicured grass. I love seeing the patterns of stripes and criss-crosses on formal lawns but it takes some work and equipment to achieve and maintain this. The good news is that a lawn can be grown with many different types of grass, it can be both formal or informal, full of wildflowers or even in a pot! Lawns don't have to be square with straight edges – in fact, creating winding paths through lawns or extending borders full of pollinating plants bringing new character to the garden are simple ways of shaking up a garden but keeping a green lawn.

A lawn isn't purely for aesthetics, though. We know that lawns absorb carbon dioxide, replacing it with oxygen and improving air quality. Lawns can also prevent flooding and erosion, cool the air and reduce pollution. They are beneficial for so many reasons: watching blackbirds find their daily breakfast of worms in the lawn is a joy, and underneath that green grass is an abundance of activity keeping your garden happy and healthy.

From Seed

Growing from seed is the cheapest way of creating a lawn, and germination occurs usually within around ten days. The ideal time for sowing lawn seed is spring or autumn. Don't forget to protect the sown seed by staking canes around the patch and covering with netting if you have pets and children who might run over it too soon (at least four weeks).

1. Clear the ground of weeds and stones.
2. If the soil is compacted, break it up to allow better root space.
3. Rake over well and level the soil as much as you can.

4. Sprinkle lawn seed where you want it to grow, following the guidelines on the packaging.
5. Lightly rake over the seed again to mix it in, making sure it has good contact with the soil. Try to get the seed as evenly spread as you can.
6. Gently water with a hose.

The key to successful germination and growth is to ensure the soil never dries out. Water the plot every day and don't step on it at all for as long as the packaging says and in any event, for at least four weeks. In the first year, keep footfall as low as possible.

From Turf

If you want instant impact, laying turf might be the best option. The best times of year for doing this are spring and autumn.

1. Clear the ground of weeds and stones.
2. If the soil is compacted, break it up.
3. Dig in some well-rotted organic matter and let it settle for a few days.
4. Rake over and level the soil (mowing a bumpy lawn is harder work!).
5. Lay turf as soon as you can after you've bought it.
6. Start in one corner of your plot and work your way to the other corner.

Avoid walking on freshly laid turf as you work and in the weeks after, to allow germination and the delicate shoots to establish. Gradually build up to gentle activity on the turf.

7. Water in by using a hose to spray water all over the turf. Try not to soak it so much that the seeds wash away but enough to penetrate the top layer of soil.
8. Water in dry weather but don't over water, ensuring the turf is not drenched all of the time – evenly moist is perfect.
9. Mow on a high setting when the grass is at least 5cm (2in) high.

Wild Lawn

A lawn doesn't have to be green grass. Wildflower lawns are extremely beneficial for pollinators and can look very pretty too. Low maintenance and adaptable, they can be grown with ease.

1. Leave a patch of grass to simply grow tall by mowing around it, or sow a packet of wildflowers where you would like them to grow.
2. Watch what grows and see what wildlife it attracts: expect to see daisies (*Bellis perennis*), buttercups (*Ranunculus acris*) or perhaps rarer plants such as the bee orchid (*Ophrys apifera*).
3. Create pathways by mowing through the centre of the wildflower lawn.

Chamomile Lawn

Roman chamomile (*Chamaemelum nobile*) creates a lawn that is not only stunning but also fragrant, great for pollinators and really low maintenance. It feels wonderfully spongy and soft under foot.

1. Remove all weeds, grass and stones from your plot.
2. Break up the soil.
3. Apply some well-rotted organic matter.
4. Plant young chamomile plants between 10 and 20cm apart.
5. Water well as soon as you have planted to ensure the plant roots get the water (not just the surface), and afterwards weekly until established.
6. No mowing needed!

Alternatively, sow Roman chamomile seeds in spring or autumn directly into well-prepared soil. Add some well-rotted organic matter into the top layer of the soil, mix sand into the top 3cm of soil and level out by raking finely. Sprinkle seeds thinly, and lightly firm in by hand or using a tamper. Then water with a fine hose. Keep moist, as with grass seed. When seedlings are at least 3cm tall, thin out to 10cm apart.

Lawn in a Pot

If you have a balcony or patio but are missing seeing grass, try growing some lawn seed in a pot. It's a lovely way to enjoy lush, green grass without an expanse of lawn, and you can even put your feet up on it or brush your fingers through the greenery. Simply sow seeds into compost in your container, water, and watch it grow. You'll need some scissors to keep the grass short, or just let it run wild and see what happens.

Small Space Gardening

I adore gardening in small spaces and getting creative with every inch available – it's such an exciting project to take on! There are so many opportunities in a petite patch to try out some unconventional gardening projects and design a really special place to fill with plants. While you may not have a huge lawn or space for a big oak tree, you will have room for dwarf tree varieties, colourful flowers and fun accessories that perhaps wouldn't work in a larger garden. Whatever the size of your plot, you can innovate and maximize the space you have to create your own garden haven.

FIVE TOP TIPS FOR SMALL SPACES

1. **Don't try to squeeze too much in.** Filling the space to the maximum with plants, furniture and accessories, will make it seem much smaller and will prove more awkward for maintenance.
2. **Big pots give maximum impact.** Just because the space is small, it doesn't mean small pots are the answer. Larger containers full of structure, texture and colour will give the wow factor.
3. **Keep up with maintenance.** Make sure you can spend a little time each week dead heading, sweeping away debris and changing up seasonal plants to keep everything looking fresh. In a small space there is nowhere to hide dead plants!
4. **Introduce shade.** If your patio is a heat trap, use tall climbers to provide some shade or plant a bamboo in a large container.
5. **Grow herbs.** These are an easy option for visual interest, attracting pollinators and using in herbal teas (see page 164 for more on how to grow herbs).

PATIO SPACE

Patios can be various sizes but, unless you want to remove it to make way for a lawn, all will involve growing in containers or raised beds. It's very easy to just look at the ground, but the most exciting part of patio gardening is the vertical space. You could simply plant up some pots and leave it at that, but if you look up and around you, a whole new world of planting opens up. From classic hanging baskets to vertical installations and pallet picture walls, there are many inexpensive options to maximize every corner of a patio space.

Planning Your Patio

Jotting your ideas down in a rough sketch first of all can be helpful in bringing your vision together.

1. Before you get started, observe where the sun and shade fall throughout the day and make a note so that you can choose the plants that will thrive best (see page 53 for more on aspect). Often, patios can have a cooler, shaded microclimate due to surrounding buildings, or, conversely, be a suntrap

without trees for shade. These factors will all impact the planting and how you use the patio.

2. Consider the style you would like. Are you happy with a simple mixture of pots and plants filling a corner? Or, would you like a theme, such as Mediterranean-style or exotic planting?
3. Think about where you want to sit – would you like a bench or bistro set? Will this be in the sun or would you prefer a shaded seating area?
4. Do you need a storage unit or garden box?
5. Look up: scan any walls or fences around you. Are they stable? Could you fit hanging basket hooks or heavier pallet planters on the walls?
6. How will you water your containers, is there a tap nearby?

BALCONY GARDENING

I have gardened on a balcony for quite a few years and while it is undoubtedly low maintenance, you can still get a great gardening fix for your green fingers. It's the perfect garden perhaps – an outdoor space needing little of your time and attention!

WATERING BALCONY CONTAINERS

Be aware that containers on a balcony need more water and feed than a garden bed because the compost dries out very quickly and the plants will use all of the nutrients as they grow. How quickly they dry out depends on the type of pot or container you are using.

Planning Your Balcony

Always start by checking the weight restrictions for your balcony and making sure that everything will be safely secured.

1. As with any other space, you need to know where the sun and shade will be throughout the day (see page 53 for more on aspect). Due to a balcony's elevated position, you'll often need to be aware of windy conditions and other inclement weather.
2. Consider the vertical spaces for more planting space. The balcony railings or wall can be used to show off your gardening accomplishments and hopefully will encourage other balcony owners to add some plants to theirs as well.
3. If there is space for a small table and chairs, think about where they will be placed and the style you would like them to be.
4. If you don't want to be watering frequently (as much as every day in the summer), then limit the number of containers you have and/or plant drought-tolerant plants. Also consider drainage: where will the water run off to? Hopefully, not down to the balcony beneath you!
5. Think of adding plants with fragrance – a lovely choice for a small space because you will be able to indulge fully in the scent. Some of my favourites are scented geranium

(*Pelargonium*), Christmas box (*Sarcococca confusa*) and star jasmine (*Trachelospermum jasminoides*) for both beauty and delectable fragrance.

6. If you would like some privacy, especially in built-up areas, you can add some screening to the inside of your balcony railings with plants such as tall bamboo.

SMALL SPACE IDEAS

There are many creative ways to make the most of a small outdoor space. Here are just a few ideas to get you started.

Grouping pots together is a way to incorporate a garden theme. Decide if you would like to grow cottage garden plants, tropical plants or edibles, for example. Before they are full of compost, move the pots around to check that you are happy with their placement.

- Creates an impact and can hide anything unsightly.
- Pots can be switched around easily and replanted seasonally.
- Use plants with similar requirements, for example, all sun loving or shade thriving.
- Create a colour scheme such as hot (red/yellow/orange) or cool (white/pink/lilac).

Dwarf fruit trees grow to about 2m (7ft) high and can be abundant with fruit in just a few years. They grow well in containers and you can choose from many fruits, from apples to pears and cherries to peaches.

- If you grow only one tree, make sure it is self-pollinating or else you will need two trees of different varieties in order to pollinate (check this before buying).
- Plant in a large container with good drainage.
- Most need plenty of sun – check the label before positioning.
- Trim the roots and repot every two to three years to give the tree enough root space to grow.

Make a home for wildlife, as well as a gorgeous addition to your small space, with a pond bucket. Imagine seeing your first dragonfly hovering around, and spotting a toad peeping up out of the water. It's quite incredible how wildlife soon find what you provide for them, even in the smallest urban spaces.

- Use a watertight container such as a washing-up bowl, a butler sink with the plug hole filled in or a tub/bucket of some kind (not too deep).
- Place stones into the bucket to make various levels for creatures to get in and out.
- Fill the pond bucket with rainwater and place some plants around the outside for wildlife to shelter and access the water.
- Add some pond plants. You'll need a mix of oxygenating, marginal and floating plants for a good balance. Oxygenators provide oxygen and places to hide for pond creatures; marginal plants provide shade and help to stop algae forming; and floating plants not only look nice but also help to provide shade and keep the water temperature cool.

Step ladders, metal racks, tables and pallets can all be used to maximize the area around you, providing more opportunities for plants. Ladder shelves and racks are a good use of vertical space and can be used for standing pots, hanging pots and displaying accessories. Standing pots on taller tables at various heights can give a new dimension to the garden and create more space for plants.

- Outdoor plant stands can be purchased in various materials.
- Visit a local car boot sale or antiques fair for bargains.
- Place a few different stands close together so that pots can be situated at various heights.
- Switch plants around or change them seasonally for something different to admire throughout the year.

Accessories can finish the look and feel of a garden, and can include items such as outdoor rugs, mirrors and lights. When you have your pots, plants and seating in place, take a look around to see if there is any space to add in accessories without making it look jumbled. Remember, whatever style you go for, it's your happy place – no matter what the theory of design will tell you. Mirrors can make the area look bigger, rugs can create the feel of seamless indoor–outdoor living and lights give a small space a magical look after dark.

- Drape string lights above your head and attach with hooks.
- If you have a wall, try creating a shape with string lights to fill the area.
- Hang string lights around taller plants.
- Twist string lights around railings or posts.

Mini greenhouses are popular, and they are good for many gardening activities. Treat a mini greenhouse as you would a standard-sized one. Place it in the sun but ventilate it on warm days, and keep a check on your plants inside. Use it to overwinter tender plants, for raising seedlings and growing vegetables.

- Make a mini greenhouse into a focal point by adding fairy lights to the shelves.
- Use it as a display cabinet for indoor plants.
- Grow trays of microgreens for a constant supply of nutrition all year round.
- Take cuttings from your existing plants and propagate them in the greenhouse for more plants (or gifts for friends).

VERTICAL GARDENING IDEAS

Another great way to make the most of a small garden space is to utilize the vertical space. Here are some of my favourite ways to incorporate vertical gardening.

Green walls are an ideal way to maximize vertical spaces and can be made in a variety of ways with different plants. They are usually created with a pre-made modular or hanging wall frame that you plant into. Some incorporate individual pots, so you can change them frequently for more planting variety.

- Ensure you safely secure a green wall structure of choice.
- Make sure you can easily water it when needed (some will come with inbuilt irrigation).
- Fill it with plants: wildflowers, annual bedding, herbs, fruit and vegetables such as strawberries and tomatoes – anything you like!
- Keep on top of dead heading and an eye out for pests and diseases.

Herb hangers are another way to use a vertical space, leaving room on the ground for more pots. Pre-made herb hangers can be bought in many different styles but they are also really easy to make, and ideal for containing the runaway roots of herbs such as mint and lemon balm.

- Measure some wire mesh with large squares to fit the size you want on the wall.
- If required, spray-paint the wire mesh to be the colour you would like.
- Screw hooks or anchors into the wall at the corners of the mesh so it can hang securely.
- Place the hooks on hanging pots with your plants onto the mesh. You can either cover the mesh entirely with plants or hang with other items such as macrame plant hangers and wind chimes.

Gutter gardens are a cheap, easy and effective way to grow plants on a wall. From one piece of guttering to a whole display, they can be used for growing plants that don't need a lot of space, such as salad leaves, small radish, peas and strawberries.

- Recycle old guttering and give it a thorough clean before drilling drainage holes along the bottom.
- Measure the lengths you would like to install and add end caps so that the compost doesn't fall out.
- Fix the guttering securely on your wall with screws.
- Fill with compost and sow your seeds!

Pallet walls are a great way to recycle old pallets and give a rustic feel to a small space. The pallets can be painted or left untreated (although you'll need to bear in mind future rot) and secured on a vertical space for planting in.

- Clean down a wooden pallet.
- Staple some good quality landscaping fabric to the back of the

pallet and line the spaces where you will plant, or create pockets to plant in using the landscaping fabric.

- Paint or decorate your pallet before you start planting, and secure to the wall with strong brackets and screws.
- Fill the pockets with compost and plant up with your choice of plants.

Macrame is back on trend and it has made it into the world of gardening, from indoor plant hangers to wall displays. Macrame plant hangers give a soft yet rustic touch outside and can be washed, replaced or brought inside over the winter. All you need is a hook to hang them from.

- Buy a macrame plant hanger kit and make one yourself – they take very little time and are a great way to relax and get crafty.
- Find a pot and plant that fits perfectly into the pot end of the hanger (anything too small will fall out).
- Fix a hook on a wall, pole or ceiling.
- Place a few hangers together for a bohemian display.

TOP TEN
PLANTS FOR BALCONIES

I love jazzing up a balcony. There is something immensely satisfying about creating a green haven in a small space, high up where you might not expect wildlife to find you. It's awe-inspiring to see your first bee land on your balcony flowers and birds visiting to take a look at what's available to enjoy. Even butterflies can make their way high up to an apartment haven, if you plant with them in mind. Often, balconies are in urban areas, so creating a wildlife friendly, green haven to enjoy in a city is so special. There's a huge diversity of plants that can be grown in containers, hanging baskets and even as a green wall. Here are my ten tried and tested favourites:

1. Bamboo

- Ideal for privacy due to height and fast growth.
- Golden or black bamboo works well.
- Plant in a large 60cm- (24in-) plus container with moist compost.
- Grows in full sun or part shade.

2. Hydrangea

- Great for a part shady area.
- Keep compost moist or they will wilt.
- Leave flower heads on for winter interest.
- Try *Hydrangea paniculata* 'Limelight' for creamy/lime flowers.

3. Sedum

- Needs well-drained soil and very little water.
- Likes sun or part shade.
- Plant a few together for an on-trend container.
- Try *Sedum* 'Atlantis', with variegated foliage and yellow flowers.

4. Succulents and cacti

- Low maintenance and thrive on neglect.
- Many can be grown outside all year.
- Use well-drained soil.
- Place in a sheltered spot with full sun.

5. Fuchsia

- Ideal for hanging baskets.
- Plant in full sun or part shade.
- Dead head regularly to prolong flowering.
- Use a peat-free multipurpose compost.

6. Mandeville

- Exotic climber with lots of flowers.
- Likes full sun to partial shade.
- Will require support to climb up.
- Well-drained, moist soil.

7. Salads

- Lettuce, rocket and mustard leaves are perfect pot plants.
- Sow direct into the soil and keep moist.
- Use a well-drained compost.
- Keep picking so they keep growing.

8. Potatoes

- Use a big pot, container or bucket.
- Fill a third with compost and lay seed potatoes on top.
- As the foliage grows keep filling with compost.
- Place in full sun.

9. Caladium

- Brightly coloured foliage plant.
- Use well-drained compost and keep moist.
- Place in a light to shady place but not full sun.
- Bring indoors before frosts and put back outside in spring.

10. Bay tree

- Easy to grow in a container.
- Use well-drained soil and water when needed.
- Pot up as it grows and prune annually to keep in shape.
- Place in a sheltered spot.

CHAPTER 3

Sourcing Plants

Getting into the nitty-gritty of gardening is undoubtedly exciting as you get your first plants in the soil or take your secateurs to a shrub for the first time. Having some tips and ideas of how to get started will set you off on your way with the knowledge you need to make the best decisions when buying plants and tools. If the various styles of plant labels baffle you when choosing your new plants, after reading this chapter you'll be able to understand the diagrams and instructions and know if they are best planted in sun or shade. Become a pro at deciphering what abbreviations mean and know how to read a seed packet, so you can sow and grow your way to a garden full of flowers and vegetables. If you wonder where to buy new garden plants, you'll find plenty of ideas in the next few pages – from the more obvious to some fun places and options, even without getting off the sofa. It's wise to know what to look out for when you are rummaging among plants in the store, so the advice across the following pages will help you to remember, even in the excitement of plant shopping, that it's a good idea to check for signs of pests or diseases on new plants before you take them home. The next time you walk in to the plant store, you will know just what to look out for.

In horticulture there are so many different types of tools, and some look and sound quite obscure! If you are wondering what loppers, a tamper or root trainers are, you'll find a handy guide to tools and accessories you might need to use as you garden and what they are used for. If you would like to keep costs to a minimum and help the environment, there are some recycled options to try, too. I really enjoy reusing and reshaping items that would generally go in the bin but instead can be cleaned up and used in the garden. It's extremely satisfying, so I hope you will try some of the suggestions and even invent some recycled tools of your own.

How to Decode a Plant Label

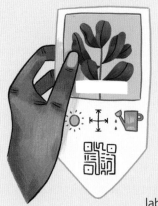

If you have ever wondered what the information on a plant label means when you find a beautiful plant at the garden centre, this guide will help you to break it all down easily. Always read the label. No matter what advice you read about a specific plant elsewhere, the label has been designed often with information directly from the breeder or grower, which will be the best advice ultimately. Save any plant labels in a safe place, at least until the plant has grown, in case you need to refer to them later to understand its requirements and remember the name!

Labels and the information given depend on the supplier and design, but each should give you a basic idea of what the plant requires, including:

Photograph – more often than not, there will be a photograph on the label that shows you what the plant will look like when fully grown with berries, flowers, fruit or vegetables. This helps you to understand exactly what to expect from the plant you are buying.

Name – the label will include the common name, variety and the botanical name. This ensures that you can't go wrong by accidentally buying the wrong plant based on the common name alone. The botanical name will usually be displayed in italics (see page 25 for more guidance on plant names).

Sun/shade – there is often a sun diagram on a plant label, which is there to advise you on the sun tolerance of the plant. This diagram will depict a half sun for part shade/sun, a full sun or a grey/empty sun for full shade. The label will also specifically say if the plant requires full sun, part shade/sun or shade. This is, perhaps, the most important instruction of all to take note of.

Mature height and spread – if the label depicts the shape of a person with measurements next to them, this is to show how tall and wide the plant will grow when mature and in comparison to the average person. This will give you a good indication of what to expect from your plant size in the future and will help you to plan accordingly.

Watering requirements – you may find water information on a label, which is usually shown with a raindrop illustration. The more raindrops there are, the more water the plant will need. More likely, the label will note how moist the soil should be kept to allow your plant to thrive. It may state any of the following:

- **Drought tolerant**, which means the plant will survive dry conditions and therefore does not like a lot of water. However, this is not necessarily the case if you grow in containers, as they will likely still need watering to a well-drained level.
- **Well drained**, which means the soil should not be heavy and should be allowed to dry out between regular watering, especially in dry weather.
- **Normal**, which means keeping the soil beneath the surface moist and only allowing the top to dry out before watering.
- **Moist**, which means keeping the soil consistently moist at all times but without overwatering.

Grafted – usually involves joining a young shoot or stem of one plant onto a stem or root of a rootstock plant (the established plant). It means the qualities from one plant, such as the flowers and fruits, can be joined to a 'stock' that grows in a required way. There are many plants available as grafted and most will say they are on the label. You will be able to see the grafting join on most towards the bottom of the plant where there is a 'bulge', which should be kept above the soil level.

Rootstock – this is the base section of a grafted plant. A plant label will refer to the rootstock using a numbering system. The rootstock determines how big the plant or tree will grow and is chosen for the desired benefits of each plant. If the label shows a rootstock number on a fruit tree, for example, it has been grafted to restrict its ultimate growth so it can be grown in a smaller space. Other benefits for growing plants on rootstocks include disease and pest resistance or longevity, fruitfulness and hardiness. The numbers shown are not suggesting which motorway your plant travelled on to get to the garden centre, they are fruit tree rootstocks identifiers!

- M27 means very dwarfing – it will fruit after 2 years and grow to a maximum of 1.8m (6ft) tall.
- M9 means dwarfing – it will fruit after 2 to 3 years and grow to a maximum of 2.4m (8ft) tall.
- M26 means semi-dwarfing – it will fruit after 2 to 3 years and grow to a maximum of 3m (10ft) tall.
- MM106 means semi-vigorous/normal – it will fruit after 3 to 4 years and grow to a maximum of 4m (13ft) tall.
- MM111 means vigorous – it will fruit after 4 to 5 years and grow to a maximum of 4.5m (15ft) tall.
- M25 means vigorous – it will fruit after 5 to 6 years and grow more than 4.5m (15ft) tall.

Patent and trademark – some labels will flag that the plant is patented and therefore cannot be propagated. A trademark symbol will also show that the name is trademark-protected by the breeder.

QR code – many labels now also include a QR code, which will take you to a factsheet about the plant when you scan it with your phone. This is an excellent way to learn more about your plant direct from the breeder or grower.

Other information – the label may provide supplementary information including further care instructions or even plant specifics including plant

spacing, tips, pest problems and
how they attract wildlife. Many
include a bee graphic,
which denotes that it is a
plant perfect for pollinators.
It might mention if the plant is
suitable for a container or a small
space. If the plant label is thorough
and understandable, you are unlikely
to need to research for any more guidance.

SEED PACKET DESCRIPTIONS

On the back of a seed packet there is usually plenty of information
to help you successfully sow and grow your seeds. This should be the
case for just about any seed packet you pick up, including perennials,
annuals, fruit and vegetables. As with plant labels, there isn't a 'one size
fits all' seed packet, so they do vary in information – some will be full of
easy-to-understand instructions and others will be more baffling. Some
won't have much information at all! This synopsis will help you to
understand what the graphics mean, so that you can get the most from
your new purchase.

The front of a seed packet may include:

- A photograph of the fully grown plant, with blooming flowers,
  berries, ripe fruit or vegetables, just as you will find on a
  plant label.
- The common name and botanical name, along with variety.
- Often, it will say if the seeds are annual, biennial or perennial.
- How many seeds are in the packet.
- A stamp to say if it is organic.
- A note stating if the seeds are heirloom (from plants that are
  at least 50 years old) or hybrid (developed by cross-breeding
  two plants for desired characteristics).

The back of a seed packet may include:

- The plant name repeated from the front.
- An imprint of the date the seeds were packaged at the bottom, along with their 'use by' date (as long as you store your seeds in a cool, dry place this date can be pushed back).
- A couple of sentences about the characteristics of the plant, such as growth rate, colour or taste.
- Sowing instruction methods, such as how far apart to sow each seed, how deep, at what time of year and how long it will take for germination.
- A useful chart showing every month of the year with colour blocks to denote when in those months you should sow, when it will flower and when you can harvest.
- A note on how many days it will take to flower or harvest from when you sow the seeds.

Other information that may appear:

- Small labels that you can detach and use to label your seeds when sown.
- A helpful note about the likely chance as a percentage of germination from sowing the seeds. For example, if 80 per cent of seeds have germinated in trials, it will say '80% germination rate'.

Where to Get Your New Plants

There are a plethora of places to buy plants, seeds, tools and gardening accessories. You will almost always be able to find the exact plant you need if you are prepared to look around and you are looking at the right time of the year. Each retailer will have different stock, as well as varying levels of service, expertise and facilities. Costs can also vary drastically between retailers, so it is always worth shopping around.

Independent Nurseries

The many benefits of shopping locally are well documented, but when you buy plants from an independent local nursery you are also likely to find a wealth of information about growing locally. Some plants will have been propagated and grown on site by horticulturalists who are experts in their field. This gives you a great opportunity to ask questions and seek advice from passionate gardeners. Independents are not just smaller garden centres, rather some are very specific about what they grow and sell. From houseplant shops to exotic outlets or singular species-only growers, there are nurseries for olive trees, topiary, orchids, carnivorous plants, bonsai and all manner of others. In these places you can really delve into the world of each plant and find rare and exciting things to grow.

Garden Centres

Some larger garden centres are family-run, some are chains and others are purely local, so this resource is a mixed bag. Many will sell not only tools and accessories but also homewares. You may find display gardens, a pet store, a cafe and even an advice centre on site. I tend to consider going to a larger garden centre as a bit of an outing because there is usually tea and cake involved! Here, you will find everything you need to grow a garden, including bulbs, herbs, perennials and annuals, shrubs and trees. You can wander along the seed racks, pick up seed trays and decide on garden lighting.

Supermarkets

It is so easy to pick up a new houseplant or pack of bedding plants as you do your weekly shop. The majority of these plants will likely grow just fine when you get them home but some won't make the mark, especially herbs. The herbs that are grown for supermarket sale aren't always kept in the best of conditions, they're rarely watered and the black plastic pots don't contain just one herb plant – they are densely packed seedlings. They are grown to last approximately two weeks while looking their best to tempt you to buy them at a cheap price. Take cuttings and root them in water to grow strong plants, or remove from the pot and separate into individual pots in the hope they will survive.

Plant Swaps

You may be able to find a local plant and seed swap where you can meet other gardeners who have plants to exchange with you. Often, you can go along even if you are completely new to gardening and don't have anything to swap. Gardeners love to chat about plants and so you can speak to others about how to garden. You might just find those seeds or that plant you've been searching for everywhere, or you might pick up a surprise plant that becomes your favourite.

Community Gardens

Not only essential for bringing people together and enhancing the local environment, community gardens are also a wonderful place to find new plants. Community gardens hold events and plant sales frequently to help with their running costs, and you will often find herbs, unusual vegetables and a variety of cuttings and seeds. Chat with the group and you might even find yourself popping down to help out sometimes and learn more about gardening while making some new friends.

Gardening Clubs

There are thousands of gardening clubs that meet up monthly. Along with the benefit of mingling with the local gardening community, many will also hold plant sales at each meeting or at events throughout the year to help fund the club. The plants are often brought in and sold by the very people who have grown them, so you will get the chance to ask lots of questions about how to grow the plants as well. The plants are typically sold at very affordable prices too!

Plant Fairs

Plant fairs are a great day out and will give you the opportunity to meet experts who grow a variety of exquisite plants. As expected with a day out plant shopping, there will likely be refreshments available and a friendly atmosphere. Stalls will include a variety of plants to buy, from bog plants to delphiniums and even local gardeners selling propagated plants from their own grounds. Never feel embarrassed to ask questions about the plants you are buying, because the sellers will want your new plants to thrive.

Garden Shows

Take a day out and attend a gardening show, where not only will you be inspired by the show gardens and floral displays but you can also bag a bargain plant or two. Nurseries bring their best plants to a garden show, which will be on sale throughout and then sold at a knocked-down price right at the very end. Make sure you take a pull-along trolley for your purchases – the temptation is strong!

Online Sellers

Buying plants online can be a tricky process as it's not always possible to be sure of what you're getting. If the seller is not specifically an online plant store, then check out the customer reviews before you order, and give feedback, especially if you do not receive what you ordered. Otherwise, stick to the more well-known and reputable online stores that sell an abundance of plant stock. You should be able to find every plant or seed you could wish for, and when they arrive at your doorstep, ready for planting, it's very exciting! Often you can pre-order so that your bulbs or plug plants will arrive at the time of year they are due to be planted out. Plug plants are young plants grown in seed cells from seed or cuttings and grown to an appropriate size for you to pot on, harden off and plant where they are to grow. This is a very cheap option if you want to grow a lot of plants at once or don't have the space for growing from seed yourself.

Car Boot Sales

I love finding plants at a car boot sale! I've even sold my own propagated plants at them. They usually start early in the morning, so rise and shine and grab a bargain. It's likely the seller has grown the plants they are selling themselves so be sure to ask lots of questions.

Online Forums

The online gardening community is thriving and always willing to help out with advice. Occasionally you will find online seed and plant swaps, or you may even find plant sales or free plants on offer when someone is moving house or has propagated too many plants.

What to Look Out for When Buying Plants

Walking into a plant shop of any kind, especially for the first time, can be overwhelming. Plants everywhere, people seemingly being experts as they shop, piles of compost to choose from – and that's before you get to the shrubs and trees. Even walking into a houseplant shop can be daunting, not knowing where to start or what to look at first. Take your time, ask questions and always read the labels. There are a few key things to look out for when you buy plants, to ensure they thrive and that you know what you are buying.

POTS

Pot sizes vary, and often the cost will depend on the size of pot. The size may be described in litres or in centimetres, and the bigger the pot, the more mature the plant. The pot size dictates the volume of soil mix that was used to grow that plant. The pot has to suit the size of the roots and plant age. Which size container plant you buy will depend on your budget, and whether you are patient enough for a young plant or want one that is already more mature for instant impact in your garden.

Most plant containers are made from black plastic, which can be used again in your garden or you can return to some stores when you have planted out. Unfortunately, black pots are not usually recyclable at local recycling centres, so are classed as single-use plastic and take hundreds of years to break down. Blue, green and red plastic pots can be recycled when cleaned. There are also recycled plastic pots and coir pots available now, which many plant sellers are starting to use.

PLANTS

A garden centre wants its plants to be in flower to entice you to buy them. This often means they have been grown to flower earlier than usual, but if it is a perennial, and you plant it out, it will grow back at the perfect time the following year. Ideally, try to buy plants that are still in bud, before they have flowered, for maximum impact in the first year.

The most popular plants are usually positioned in the most prominent places so that you can find them easily. You will also find plants conveniently organized into groups such as perennials, bedding plants, shrubs and trees.

Yellow or brown leaves can be a sign of incorrect watering (too much or too little), a nutrient deficiency or incorrect light levels. Often they can be brought back to full beauty with some tender love and care, but sometimes it can be tricky. Decide if you want to take on that challenge before purchasing. If the leaves are simply wilting, it means the plant is in need of a thorough water and will usually perk up if it hasn't been left too long.

Root-bound plants (also described as pot bound) are those that have been growing in their pot for so long that the roots are poking out of the drainage holes. This happens if the plant hasn't had the correct levels of water, nutrition or general care. The roots inside the pot will be circling, look dense and it might even be tricky to remove the plant from the pot. Check by gently lifting the plant to see the root ball – if all you can see are the roots, then it's root bound. Roots can be loosened by teasing them apart before planting in the garden, or more tenacious roots can be sliced (plants can be far tougher than we give them credit for). However, generally, if you buy a root-bound plant, they will get off to a slow start and may not thrive in the long run.

You may spot little plants growing in the compost of a new container plant. These could well be weeds, grabbing a ride to your garden.

They usually won't cause any problems, just make sure that you pull them out before you take your new plants home or place your new plant in your garden. Some weeds can be persistent, so make sure you don't miss any. They will be better off in the compost bin.

PESTS AND DISEASES

Introducing a new plant to your house or garden can, unfortunately, bring with it any number of pests or diseases both inside and outside. There is nothing more disheartening than bringing home your perfect plant to find it covered in pests, which then infect other plants. Give the plant you are looking at a full inspection, and look out for these warning signs before you buy:

- **Leaves** – if you see any yellow, brown, spotty or mottled foliage this could be a sign of a pest infestation. Many pests tend to hide under the leaves or in places where you have to seek them out. There may be holes or noticeable munching signs, which is a very clear sign that pests are present.
- **Abnormal or distorted growth** – this means there could be an aphid infestation. A severe aphid infestation can stunt the growth of plants and you will most likely be able to see little green, black or white bugs. If the bugs have been treated but the plant still looks unwell, that's another sign to step away.
- **Other obvious signs of pests** – red spider mites are tiny but they can be spotted by the webbing they spin on a plant. Scale insects leave a sticky residue on the plant and look like tiny bumps. Fungus gnats are tiny white wriggly bugs that will appear if you disturb an infected houseplant. They can be a real pain as they lay their eggs in the compost and feed off the plant roots.

What Tools Do You Need and What Are They Used For?

It is unquestionably easier to garden when you have the right tools and understand what they are best used for. There are many recycling tricks to help you out, if you can't get hold of the traditional tools or objects. Store your tools in a cool, dry place and wipe them down as often as you can (ideally after use) to keep them in good condition and to help stop the spread of pests and diseases. Don't panic if you don't have time for that though – I clean mine about once each season. You certainly don't need all of these tools, so select what is appropriate for the amount of gardening you will be doing and the space you have to use them on.

TOOLS TO CONSIDER

Bulb planter – digs holes in the soil to plant bulbs easily and then put the soil back on top of the bulbs.

Dibber – for making holes in the ground or pots of compost to sow seeds or transplant seedlings.

Fork – for mulching, forking in compost and the all-important potato harvest.

Garden rake – used to move soil, dead materials, grass, break up clods of soil and level out the soil.

Grass trimmer – for cutting grass and edging the lawn.

Hand fork – great for removing weeds, lifting small plants and levelling soil around plants.

Hedging shears – looking like large scissors, these are used to trim and shape hedging. They can also be used to cut back perennials and anything else needed.

Hoe – can be used for light weeding, loosening the soil and even making seed drills for sowing.

Leaf rake – a larger looking rake than the garden rake, this is used to scoop away fallen leaves from the lawn or garden beds.

Loppers – with two handles, these are used for pruning medium branches.

Pruning saw – turn to these for pruning larger stems and branches when neither secateurs or loppers are big enough.

Secateurs (also known as pruners) – for pruning plants, dead heading and for removing smaller stems and branches.

Shovel – shaped differently to a spade with a more rounded shape, a shovel is used for digging, shovelling, moving and lifting plants.

Spade – mainly used for gentle cultivation, digging in mulch or digging holes for larger plants.

Strimmer – cuts grass and weeds, and even perennials if they aren't too big.

WHAT TOOLS DO YOU NEED AND WHAT ARE THEY USED FOR?

Tamper – with a long handle and a heavy flat base, this tool is used to level the ground.

Trowel – an ideal tool for container gardening and light tasks when you might be transplanting, sowing seeds and digging smaller holes.

ACCESSORIES

Grow lights – if you grow indoors, these are good for young plants, houseplants and even homegrown vegetables. They are used to cultivate plants all year round.

tamper

Module trays – used to sow one or two seeds per module, allowing growth until transplanting.

Propagator – like a mini greenhouse for seedlings, this usually consists of a tray to sow into and a transparent plastic cover to keep seeds warm. There is usually a vent to control the temperature.

Root trainers – used to grow plants that need deep root space, such as sweet peas (*Lathyrus odoratus*).

Seed trays – used to sow multiple seeds into compost until the seedlings are ready to be thinned out or transplanted.

plastic-bottle
cloche

RECYCLED OPTIONS

Food trays – collect food trays, drinks cartons and anything that has space for compost and seeds to grow. Make sure you can make drainage holes, and treat them just the same as seed trays.

Pencil – this can be used instead of a dibber for sowing seeds or to lift seedlings when thinning out (see page 159).

Plastic containers or bottles – you can use these as cloches to protect young plants from weather and pests.

Recycled bottles – punch holes in the lid of a bottle and fill with water for a homemade watering can.

Stone markers and corks on forks – paint stones and put corks on old forks to mark where you have sown seeds or planted new plants.

Toilet roll tubes – the central cardboard roll can be used instead of root trainers or cut in half to be used instead of module trays.

There are other tools, variations and accessories made specifically for ease and comfort of use. Find the tools that you feel comfortable with, keep them in good shape, and your gardening time will be more effective and enjoyable.

HOW TO GROW A TREE

'To plant a garden is to believe in tomorrow' – Audrey Hepburn

Planting a tree is one of the most satisfying jobs in the garden. Trees are the lungs of our planet, creating oxygen for all living species on Earth. As you dig the soil ready to plant a new tree in your garden, you might think about how important this process is for your local environment, the planet and future generations.

Before you plant a new tree, carefully consider the species, the size it will ultimately grow to and the maintenance it will need over the years to come. With proper care, healthy trees provide homes and food for wildlife and are a beautiful sight to behold. Choose trees that have nectar-rich flowers for insects, berries for birds and plentiful places for nesting. Fruit trees will, of course, provide an abundance of homegrown goodness, and many can be grown in containers.

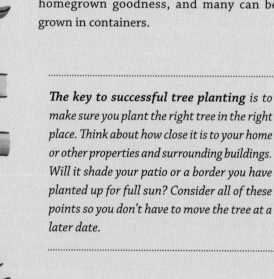

The key to successful tree planting *is to make sure you plant the right tree in the right place. Think about how close it is to your home or other properties and surrounding buildings. Will it shade your patio or a border you have planted up for full sun? Consider all of these points so you don't have to move the tree at a later date.*

Planting Container-Grown Trees

The best time of year to plant trees is from November to March, when they are dormant. This gives the roots time to establish before the warmer weather in late spring and throughout summer.

1. Remove the tree from the pot you have bought it in and place the root ball into a bucket of water to thoroughly soak while you prepare the planting hole.
2. Dig a hole approximately three times the width of the root ball and to the same depth as the pot.
3. Gently loosen the compost and roots on the root ball before planting – this will help the roots to establish.
4. Place the tree into the hole and make sure the top of the bottom part of the trunk where it meets the root ball is level with the surface.
5. Most young trees will need staking, so place a stake into the hole.
6. Fill the hole in with the soil you have dug out and thoroughly water it in.
7. Use tree support tape to tie the tree to the stake.
8. Mulch the ground around the tree, leaving about a 10cm (4in) gap from the trunk (see page 186 for further information on mulching).

Aftercare

Once the tree is planted, keep it well watered until it is fully established – this can take a year or two. Newly planted trees should be watered daily for a week or so, then approximately three times a week (and sometimes more in dry, warm weather) for around five or six weeks, when you can start to water it once a week. If the tree canopy isn't covering the ground beneath it, you might get a break from watering in heavy rainfall, but continue to water in light rain because it's unlikely to reach the roots.

Planting Bareroot Trees

These are trees that are sold without any soil around the roots. They are cheaper to buy, easier to transport and establish really well with the right care. When planting bareroot trees, the key is watering. As the roots have no attachment to soil they will need plenty of moisture to establish, so daily watering is essential, even if it's raining lightly. These are generally available in the winter, and will also include many perennials, shrubs and roses.

TREES FOR SMALL SPACES

If you only have a small garden or outside space, you can still incorporate a tree. Try any of the following tree species, which should thrive in a small space.

- **Serviceberry/Juneberry** *(Amelanchier lamarckii)* is a small tree with star-shaped flowers in spring and pinkish leaves. During summer, the leaves will be green and later turn red, which makes for some beautiful visual interest most of the year. The berries in summer are great for wildlife, and it can be easily grown in well-drained soil from full sun to part shade. Pollinators will love it.
- **Peach 'Avalon Pride'** *(Prunus persica* **'Avalon Pride')** is a pretty, small tree with pink flowers. Plant in a warm, sunny and sheltered place ensuring it is not subject to late frosts, as they can damage the flowers and subsequent fruits. The taste of home-grown peaches is exquisite!
- **Rowan 'Rosiness'** *(Sorbus rosea* **'Rosiness')** is loved by garden birds for its pretty leaves, spring flowers and autumn berries. Plant in full sun or light shade and in well-drained soil.
- **Common hawthorn** *(Crataegus monogyna)* is a wonderful tree planted alone or as a hedge to support wildlife. With pretty white flowers and red berries, the hawthorn is incredibly easy to grow. Plant in full sun with well-drained soil and watch the birds flock to your garden.

Don't forget to hug your tree!

(See Planting in Pots and Hanging Baskets, page 141, for container trees.)

CHAPTER 4

Planting into Soil

From smaller spaces filled with vegetables growing in pots and hanging baskets packed full of colourful bedding plants to new gardens in need of a makeover, you'll find a lot of useful information here so that you can make the most of your garden. If you've ever walked into a plant shop and been confused at the various styles and materials that pots are made from, you'll find a guide covering the pros and cons of each. As always, there are some recycled options for both containers and hanging baskets, so before you throw anything out, get creative and see if you can use it in the garden. With ideas for planting combinations, the top ten vegetables to grow and the all-important plants for pollinators that are ideal for pots and containers, I hope it will enthuse you to embrace plants in every corner of your garden.

If you haven't heard of no-dig gardening, it's time to get your gardening geek on, because no dig is back with a bang. The environmental impact of gardening is crucial, so understanding the dig versus no-dig methods of gardening is essential to enable you to make an informed decision. From understanding these methods to deciding if raised-bed gardening might be helpful for you and encouraging wildlife in as you garden, the following pages are packed full of information.

When you have prepared your soil, built your raised beds and put your plans together, it's time to start sowing seeds and planting out. You'll be sprinkling tiny seeds of hope in trays of compost with information on how to sow, thin out, harden off and planting. This includes which type of growing medium to use and options for seed trays including recycled items from the home. And if you are wondering what time of year sowing and growing should ideally happen, this chapter covers when trees, vegetables, fruit and flowers can be sown or planted out. This will give you a good idea of what to plan for in each season, so you can be well prepared to make the most of the time you have to garden, and create a space full of plants and wildlife.

Planting in Pots and Hanging Baskets

Whether your garden is large or small, pots and hanging baskets can be a useful addition to grow fruit, vegetables and ornamentals. They're also perfect for patios and balconies, to maximize the space available, and are ideal for creating a personalized vibe.

If you are renting your home or would prefer plants requiring little maintenance, pots, containers and hanging baskets can be an easy way to spruce up your space. With so many pot and plant choices, you can design an area in exactly the style you choose. Even though there may be less to do by gardening this way, it is worth thinking about what you would like your pots to look like before rushing to get started, or you'll end up with a patio of pots not looking quite how you had imagined.

CONTAINER OPTIONS

From choosing colours to materials, your container choices will have a big effect on the ease of use, health of your plants and overall style of your garden.

Terracotta pots are porous, which allows for water and air to penetrate through – this is good for preventing diseases and root rot. However, they are heavy to move and can crack in cold weather. If you won't need to move them around much, they are a good choice, and they work well for plants that don't need much water. Fibrecotta is an imitation of terracotta but much lighter and frost proof.

Glazed ceramic can be found in many colours and patterns, so you will likely find some to suit your style. They can be heavy to move, though, and expensive to purchase.

Metal pots look sharp and modern but also greatly absorb heat, resulting in your plants sitting in an oven-like environment. They can rust and some can also be heavy. Galvanized steel is treated with zinc to limit rust, so check the label to see if this is the case.

Plastic (not the black plastic pots that plants are sold in) is durable, light and generally inexpensive. Try to purchase pots made from recyclable plastic that can be recycled again, to limit environmental damage. Some plastic pots are self-watering and are available with pot trays attached. There are more environmentally friendly options now becoming available for home gardeners, such as pots made from recycled ocean plastic and bamboo.

Wood planters fit in with most garden styles and give a natural look, but they can crack in cold weather. They can be slow to dry out after a wet spell and very heavy. Wooden containers can also rot easily, and it is helpful to line them with some horticultural fabric.

Fabric/grow bags are lightweight and easy to store when not in use. They are available in different sizes and colours but most won't last more than a couple of years and may disintegrate if left outside over the winter months.

Resin planters are durable and available in many shapes, sizes and colours. They look like stone but don't weigh as much. They are easy to keep clean and will last for years, making them a cost-effective option.

Recycled pots and reused containers are fun to find and use, and will add a touch of quirkiness to your small space. You can try a variety of different materials.

POLLINATOR PLANTS FOR POTS AND CONTAINERS

There are so very many plants to choose from that are attractive to pollinators! You can find a comprehensive list on many wildlife and gardening websites. Here are some of my favourites:

1. *Erysimum cheiri* 'Scarlett Bedder' (Wallflower)
2. *Lavandula angustifolia* 'Peter Pan' (Lavender)
3. *Thymus vulgaris* 'Old English' (Thyme)
4. *Hylotelephium takesimense* 'Atlantis' (Sedum)
5. *Salvia* × *sylvestris* 'Caradonna' (Salvia)
6. *Gerbera jamesonii* 'Fundy'
7. *Nepeta nervosa* 'Blue Moon' (Catmint)
8. *Helleborus orientalis* 'Hello Pearl' (Lenten Rose)
9. *Pulmonaria* 'Blue Ensign' (Lungwort)
10. *Echinacea* 'Green Twister' (Coneflower)

Recycled Containers

From antique yards to online forums, there is always a bargain to be found for the garden, and some of the most exquisite containers I have ever seen have been picked up from car boot sales or found abandoned at the back of an overgrown garden. Some containers can be expensive, so taking time to salvage unique items for upcycling means you will not only save some money but you will also be able to say you have a one-of-a-kind pot in your garden!

Butler sinks are a classic upcycled garden container. Leave the plug hole open for drainage, fill with a peat-free multipurpose compost and plant up. Alternatively, fill in the plug hole and make a patio pond bucket (see page 93).

Tea cups can be used for a fun table display – plant up with some succulents or alpine plants. They need very little water, and it's a great way to reuse old cups and saucers. Alternatively, glue a cup to the saucer on its side and fill with bird seed. The seed will spill onto the saucer for the birds to easily find. Hang it up from a wall or in a tree.

Old dustbins have an ideal depth for growing potatoes, horseradish, parsnips, carrots and even dwarf fruit trees. They can be cleaned out and then left bare or painted, so you can be as creative as you want.

Used tyres can be ideal for filling in the centre with compost and planting crops such as strawberries, wildflowers or creating seasonal displays. If you pile tyres on top of each other and fill with compost, you'll have a fun, raised bed that can also be painted.

A chest of drawers creates a more unconventional planter. Upcycle an old set of drawers by drilling drainage holes in each drawer, then line with some horticultural material and fill with compost ready to plant up. Leave the bottom drawer fully open and each higher drawer slightly more closed. This is perfect for growing microgreens, salads, bedding plants and herbs.

VEGETABLE PLANTS

Just like plants for pollinators, there's lots of vegetables that can be grown in containers. These are my top ten:

1. Runner bean 'White Lady'
2. Swiss chard 'Celebration'
3. Potato 'Charlotte'
4. Rhubarb 'Champagne'
5. Spring onion 'White Lisbon'
6. Tomato 'Atlas'
7. Carrot 'Chantaney'
8. Radish 'Sparkler'
9. Kale 'Redbor'
10. Aubergine 'Black Beauty'

HANGING BASKETS

A lavish hanging basket with
cascades of flowers is one of the
prettiest sights in a garden. Incredibly
easy to keep looking lush all summer
with some easy maintenance tips, they are
the ideal space saver and can be home to
various different plants, fruit and vegetables.

There are many different types of hanging baskets to choose from but
it is the size that is particularly important. If you pack out a hanging
basket with too many plants for its size, it will dry out quickly and you'll
be watering constantly in an attempt to keep the plants thriving. To
grow a big ball of beautiful blooms, you'll need to plant up a larger-
sized basket so there is enough root space. A rough guide of 12 annual
plants per 30cm (12in) basket is a good measure to go by, except when
you are growing one large plant such as a fern. For larger plants such
as geraniums and fuchsias, stick to five plants per 30cm (12in) basket.
However, as with gardening in general, use your judgement and see
how it goes. Care for your baskets in the same way as containers –
keep them watered, well fed and don't stop dead heading!

*Cut some slits in the liner around the outside of your basket, and plant
into these holes as well as in the top space. This will make your baskets
look lavishly full.*

PLANTS FOR HANGING BASKETS

Petunias, surfinia, bacopa, calibrachoa, nasturtiums, bidens, begonias, verbena and lobelia can all be mixed together to create a beautiful hanging basket, along with many others. However, some of the most vibrant displays are made from filling a basket with one variety for a big wow factor. Some perfect combinations in a hanging basket are:

- *Petunia* Frills and Spills 'Darcey Rosa' and *Bacopa* 'Snowtopia'
- *Pelargonium* 'Oldbury Duet', trailing lobelia 'Waterfall Blue Ice' (*Lobelia erinus*) and *Petunia* 'Trailing Surfinia Hot Pink'
- *Calibrachoa* 'Million Bells Red', *Verbena* 'Vectura White' and *Antirrhinum nanum* 'Frosted Flames'
- African daisy 'Falling Stars' (*Osteospermum*), Cape jewels 'Tapestry' (*Nemesia strumosa compacta*) and *Dianthus* 'White'
- *Geranium* 'Ville de Paris White', *Coleus* 'Walter Turner' and busy lizzie 'Sun Harmony' (*New Guinea impatiens*)
- Chilli peppers and nasturtiums

Tumbling tomatoes, strawberries, chilli peppers, as well as many salad leaves can also be grown in hanging baskets and containers.

Upcycled Hanging Baskets

Using recycled materials in the garden provides endless fun and creativity, and you can use many different old household items to display hanging plants. These are great projects to get children involved in the garden, too.

Colanders can be hung up with wire or on chains attached to the colander handles with carabiner clips. Fill with compost and plant up with herbs or annuals.

Drinks bottles don't have to be thrown away as they have multiple uses in the garden, from plant protection to hanging displays. Cut the bottle in half and keep the cap on. Turn it upside down, punch some drainage holes in the sides and fill with compost. Plant up and hang with string. You can even connect them so three or more hang above one another.

Wellies with holes in are no good for wearing but perfect for planting! Make plenty of drainage holes, fill with compost and plant in the top. Multiple wellies, side by side on a wall, can brighten up any garden.

Tin cans are perfect for potting and displaying herbs in, and you can paint them in bright colours or write the plant names on the outside of the tins. Clean them out after use, make holes in the bottom for drainage and at the top for strong string to be threaded through. Plant up and hang around your garden.

CONTAINER AND HANGING BASKET CARE

There are a few maintenance jobs you will need to attend to in order to ensure your newly planted containers and hanging baskets grow and flourish.

Watering

Remember, most importantly, that pots and hanging baskets will need frequent watering, so ensure you can get a water source to them easily. They will dry out quickly, especially in hot weather, so be prepared to water daily if necessary. You might find that one minute everything looks fine and the next all of the foliage is wilting. Keeping to a watering schedule can be useful – early mornings or later in the evening are the best times, to allow the plants to absorb the water before it all evaporates. If you have a slug or snail problem, watering in the morning might be better because slugs enjoy the dampness at night when they are most active. Also, it's worth noting that it's much better to soak containers all the way through rather than watering little and often. The latter doesn't give the roots much chance to absorb the water. With any plants, it's also better to water directly into the soil/compost rather than over the plant, because it helps to prevent diseases and means the water is getting directly to the roots, where it is needed.

Feeding

As your plants grow, they take up the nutrients from the compost. When all of those nutrients have been used, what happens next? If the plants aren't given a balanced feed, they will likely decline and you'll have to start all over again. Many composts will have a slow-release fertilizer mixed in, which will last for about a month. Always check the packaging for exact timings and to make sure it is organic. After that, you will need to keep feeding your containers from spring onwards, throughout summer. There are many options to choose, from seaweed liquid feed to homemade comfrey and nettle feed and other fertilizers (see page 186). There is some debate over the benefit of fertilizers and their overall impact on the planet, so do your research when deciding which to buy and/or use.

Dead Heading

Snip off those flower heads as soon as you notice they have gone past their best, if you want to prolong flowering and get more blooms. Alternatively, leave them to go to seed if you want to collect seeds or provide interest and food over the colder months. Cutting off the flower heads will give your plants more energy for producing additional flowers.

Having some decent, sharp secateurs will make the job much quicker and easier. Also, snip off any dead or diseased material as and when to keep plants looking healthy. (See Dead Heading, page 211.)

Seasonal Planting

If you are gardening solely in containers or with hanging baskets, the seasons are just as important as if you were growing in a large garden. You can plant for each season, shake things up as the weather changes and have beautiful plants all year round to appreciate. In the spring and summer it's all about dead heading, watering and feeding; but autumn and winter are very different seasons. (See The Gardening Year at a Glance, page 222.)

In autumn, you'll need to start preparing your pots and hanging baskets for the winter months ahead. Remove old summer bedding plants, prune out dead material and generally give them a tidy and mulch. If you have tender perennials or tropical plants growing, move them inside by a window with bright light. Half-hardy perennials can be moved to a shed, garage or unheated greenhouse. Otherwise, grouping pots together in a sheltered place can be beneficial for insulation, and even wrapping them with horticultural fleece or saved packaging material such as bubble wrap can help. Terracotta and ceramic pots can crack when frozen so wrap them, or empty the contents into your compost pile and store them upside down and inside over winter.

By winter, it can be helpful to lift your containers up onto pot feet or bricks, which will help with drainage after heavy rainfall. If there is a long dry spell, you might even need to water your pots if they dry out, but never do this if it's freezing, and ideally water during the day when the soil has warmed up a little from overnight low temperatures. Many perennials, shrubs and trees need to have a cold season to ensure they will flower the following year, so it's perfectly fine to leave these outside (unless the label on the plant you bought says otherwise). Hanging baskets can be planted up with winter bedding plants, but I do tend to move them into the shed for protection. Keeping them out of the harsh winter weather can help with longevity and ensure they don't blow around, break or even fall down. It's then exciting to bring them back out again to plant up during the following spring.

You can rotate your containers or baskets if they aren't too heavy, to allow for bushy, even growth from all sides. That way, all plants will get plenty of sun from every angle.

SMALL TREES

What is a garden without a tree? Thankfully many dwarf varieties are available and many others grow perfectly well in a big container. Try any of the following:

1. Eastern redbud (*Cercis canadensis* 'Eternal Flame')
2. Dwarf crab apple (*Malus toringo* 'Aros')
3. Japanese maple (Acer palmatum 'Osakazuki')
4. Weeping cherry (*Prunus* 'Kiku-shidare-zakura')
5. Dwarf fig (*Ficus carica* 'Majoam' Little Miss Figgy)
6. Star magnolia (*Magnolia stellata* 'Royal Star')
7. Pink flowering dogwood (*Cornus florida* f. *rubra*)
8. Silk tree (*Albizia julibrissin* 'Summer Chocolate')
9. Witch hazel (*Hamamelis* × *intermedia* 'Jelena')
10. Jacaranda tree (*Jacaranda mimosifolia* 'Bonsai Blue')

TOP TEN
LOW-MAINTENANCE PLANTS

Low-maintenance plants are most gardeners' dream, especially if you want to dress up your garden but have little time to spare. Fewer watering, feeding and pruning requirements mean less time needed to keep plants thriving. Generally, the least maintenance comes from ensuring the right plant for the right place and avoiding notorious 'diva' plants. Thankfully, there are plenty of plants for the low-maintenance garden, and these are some of my favourites:

1. Daylily 'Red Precious' (*Hemerocallis* 'Red Precious')

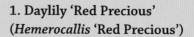

- Tough plant that flowers throughout summer.
- Doesn't mind being neglected.
- Each flower lasts one day with many blooms.
- Plant in full sun.

2. Snapdragon 'La Bella Pink' (*Antirrhinum majus* 'La Bella Pink')

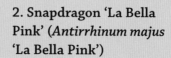

- Long flowering season.
- Requires little watering.
- Pink, butterfly-shaped flowers.
- Plant in full sun.

3. Geranium [Rozanne]
(*Geranium* Rozanne 'Gerwat'[PBR])

- Hardy plant with a long flowering season.
- Water in dry weather.
- Great for the front of borders and ground cover.
- Plant in full sun but does tolerate part shade.

4. Courgette
(*Cucurbita pepo* 'Defender' F1)

- Reliable variety that grows vigorously.
- Produces abundant crop of dark green, tender courgettes.
- Flowers in summer, so ideal for borders.
- Plant in full sun and water as needed.

5. *Mangave* 'Inkblot'

* Cross between *Agave* and *Manfreda*.
* Interesting patterned leaves.
* Needs very little water.
* Plant in well-drained soil.

6. Ice plant (*Delosperma cooperi* 'Jewel of Desert')

* Drought tolerant, little water needed.
* Low growing, great for ground cover,
  containers or borders.
* Vibrant pink flowers.
* Grow in full sun, well-drained soil.

7. Butterfly bush 'Sungold' (*Buddleja* × *weyeriana* 'Sungold')

* A magnet to pollinators.
* Clusters of yellow, fragrant flowers.
* Will grow anywhere.
* Water when establishing.

8. African daisy (*Osteospermum* 'Sunny Mary')

- Vibrant purple flowers.
- Flowers throughout summer.
- Protection needed in winter.
- Plant in well-drained soil, in full sun.

9. Avens 'Totally Tangerine' (*Geum* 'Totally Tangerine'[PBR])

- Flowers for months in summer.
- Great for the front of borders.
- Grows well in containers.
- Plant in full sun or part shade.

10. Skimmia (*Skimmia* × *confusa* 'Kew Green')

- Evergreen glossy leaves.
- Fragrant white flowers in spring.
- Grows in part or full shade.
- Plant in neutral to acidic soil.

How to Make a New Garden Bed

It's exciting to get started on creating a new garden bed, and despite what you may have read about killing off grass or digging out turf, it can actually be a whole lot easier than that. If you are looking for a major workout, then digging out turf is definitely high on the scale for calorie burning but is also unnecessarily hard on your back, and the soil. The easiest way to create a new bed is to follow the 'no dig' method. There are many ways to make a new garden bed from raised wooden or metal frames and even straw bales.

DIG OR NO DIG

Digging is how we have been taught to garden for a very long time. It can include rotivating (turning the soil over with machinery) and double digging, which is a method to create a deep bed of loose soil that improves drainage and aeration. However, digging soil can have a negative impact ultimately on its structure over time, which can mean a loss of moisture retention and nutrients. Digging also earths up weeds and seeds, so it can be counter-productive.

No-dig gardening sounds unconventional but it is actually as nature intended. Leaves fall from trees, land on the ground and replenish the soil. It's an organic process where the soil isn't turned over between growing crops in a vegetable garden, and in an ornamental garden it is simply replenishing the soil each year where your plants grow. Earthworms help to take the mulch down into the soil, which helps to improve soil structure and drainage. The millions of other soil organisms break down the mulch, which releases food for plants. There simply isn't any digging required.

If you choose to garden in a no-dig style, the soil will still be disturbed when you plant and harvest, but this will be much less disruption than if you dig. With no dig, you will see far less weeds as the soil is not disturbed, so weeds do not get to the surface as they are suppressed under the layer of mulch. Of course, there will be some weeds blown in the wind that will land on the surface of the mulch or soil, so hoeing them away as they appear is the best way to keep them in check.

If your soil is compacted or completely void of nutrients to start with, you could use a combination of the two methods. Turning the soil, forking in lots of well-rotted organic matter, raking it over level and then layering cardboard/paper before mulching can be helpful.

CREATING YOUR NEW BED

The best time to make a new bed is from October to March. That way you will have all winter to let your new bed settle, then plants bulbs, perennials and sow seeds ready for the following year.

1. Firstly, find out if there are any cables or pipes underground so you can avoid them.
2. Get started with a hose or a bucket of sand. Lay the hose where you would like the edge of the bed to be, and move it around until you are happy with the shape and size. Either leave the hose there when you start to make your bed or mark the edge with sand then move the hose out of the way.
3. Remove any tenacious weeds with big roots in the area, such as brambles and docks. If the soil is full of stones or other debris, remove as much as you can. Don't worry about any small weeds or grass if you are going for a no-dig bed. You can mow the grass first, or not bother! If you want to turn the soil and dig, you'll need to clear everything out of the bed.
4. Either create the edge of the bed by digging a little trench with a spade or alternatively simply place a thick layer of cardboard over the space then layer a good 10–15cm (4–6in) of well-rotted compost directly on top of the cardboard. The cardboard will help to block out light and therefore kill off any weeds and grass. Over the winter months, the paper will break down, the rain and worms will help the nutrients from the compost absorb into the soil and you will be ready to start planting.
5. Tidy the edges when the bed is formed and settled over the coming months. Stomp on it or use a tamper to firm the compost down and you have a bed ready – just like that!

Whether you are growing ornamentals or vegetables, I would recommend planting trees and shrubs before you layer the cardboard/paper and compost, as the bigger roots can settle in and it saves you having to dig a big hole through the mulch and cardboard at a later date. Some gardeners plant directly into the new bed straight away, but I prefer to wait a few weeks for it to settle before I plant anything else and for the cardboard/paper to break down a little. If you would like to sow seeds direct into a new no-dig bed, use some fine compost on the top layer of your bed and sow into that to help seeds germinate.

Dig or no dig, each year replenish your soil with a layer of mulch. With a no-dig bed, there's no need to dig this into the top layer of soil, you simply add it to the top and let nature take its course.

RAISED BED OR IN-GROUND PLANTING

Gardens big or small can benefit from raised beds for a variety of reasons. There are so many options available in terms of size, shape and materials, that you can create a specific style of garden just from raised beds and never dig into the ground at all. Raised beds are helpful if your ground is extremely compacted or if you have a small space, balcony or patio. They are also easy to access and so less stressful on your back and knees. The soil won't become compacted, will have better drainage and can even prevent some pests getting to your precious plants (the carrot root fly, for example, doesn't fly above 60cm/24in, so your carrots will be safe!). The compost in a raised bed tends to warm up earlier than soil in the ground and stays warm longer, which means you can extend your growing season as well. This is especially good for salads and vegetables.

In-ground planting has plenty of benefits too, so it really is a personal choice depending on your space and preference. Creating a new bed in the ground can mean less watering, especially if you are growing in a warmer climate. There are no upfront costs of buying the materials and putting the beds together, and it is easier to create shaped beds exactly where you want them to be in the ground.

MAKE SPACE FOR WILDLIFE

Encouraging wildlife into your garden is the best way to create a biodiverse ecosystem full of wonder and interest. Not only is a wildlife haven good for your garden, local environment and the planet but also for your own wellbeing[1]. It's joyous to watch birds bathing, toads hopping and butterflies fluttering around your garden, so keep your binoculars by the window to see what's going on outside. Make space in your new bed or by your raised beds with these wildlife friendly ideas:

A wood pile provides home, shelter and food for many garden creatures. Pile old branches, twigs, leaves, hollow plant stems and moss together, and see which species the decomposing wood attracts to your patch.

Building an insect hotel to place in your new garden bed will provide a space for many garden insects. There are DIY kits available to build, pre-made hotels or plenty of instructional videos online to help you make your own. Collect lots of natural material to use in your hotel rooms to make their stay comfortable, such as straw, moss, bark, bamboo, dry leaves and stones.

Sinking a small pond into your bed can attract toads, frogs, newts and other water creatures in no time at all. Even a pond the size of a washing-up tub is big enough to create a wildlife pond. (See making a pond bucket, page 93.)

Make sure your beds are perfect for pollinators by planting hedging instead of fencing where possible and trees with berries to support the local bird population. Supplementary food and water is also important – try to make space for a bird table, bird bath or bird feeders on stakes that complement the style of your new garden bed.

Sowing and Growing

When your containers or beds are prepared, the all-important stage of growing begins. It still never ceases to amaze me how tiny seeds grow into huge pumpkins and bulbs burst through the soil to bring so much joy in spring. From sowing seeds to knowing which way up to plant a bulb, you'll need some simple tips to help you get growing.

It's important to sow into clean pots, trays, modules or recycled containers. Give everything a wash with warm soapy water and rinse before using them. This will help to stop the spread of disease.

GROWING MEDIUM

There are different types of growing medium for sowing and growing from seed. Trial and error is often the way, and here are the common mediums to use:

Seed compost is produced to be the ideal texture – it's light and low in nutrients. The seed has the energy it needs to grow within itself but needs steady levels of air, light, moisture and warmth to survive and grow strong. Seed compost will help to maintain these levels.

Multipurpose compost is high in nutrients, which can be detrimental to seed germination. It can be used to sow seeds but can work better for larger seeds. However, don't be put off if that's all you can get hold of – I have used it for sowing successfully many times! To make it finer, you can sieve it into your seed tray.

Coco coir is made from the fibre found between the husk and outer shell of a coconut. Coir can be used for sowing seeds as it's moisture retentive, so you won't need to water as much as if you sow into compost.

Vermiculite as a natural mineral is sterile and moisture retentive, making the finer grade vermiculite great for germinating seeds in. If you mix it with potting compost, you'll have a great medium for sowing seeds.

SOWING METHODS

Before you start sowing, check the seed packet for the use-by date. If the packet is out of date, the germination rate may be less. You can still give it a go, often seeds are still good to grow long after the date, but just be aware that you might need to start again if you don't get enough to germinate. Always follow the seed packet instructions, but as a general guide, the following methods should work well.

Small seeds, such as salads, can be scattered thinly onto the surface of moist compost and pressed down gently. Some will need a fine layer of compost on top, others can be left on the surface. If you water after sowing, the water might wash the seeds around or even push them too deeply into the soil. For smaller seeds use a mister spray to keep the soil evenly moist but not overwatered. Place the seed trays in a warm area without direct sunlight or draughts and keep a check on them daily.

One way to keep your seeds moist is to use a propagator tray. This is a tray into which you sow seeds as normal, with a clear lid that locks in the moisture and a vent on top to ensure it doesn't get too hot inside. Otherwise, don't let seedlings dry out but don't flood them with water either. Keep a check on the soil and try to keep it evenly moist at all times.

Tiny seeds shouldn't be sown too thickly or all poured in to one spot. To avoid this, try mixing the seed with sand before sowing or making your own seed paper. Mix one part of water with four parts of flour into a paste, then take strips of kitchen paper, dot the paste on at regular intervals along the paper (according to the spacing instructions on the packet) and drop a couple of seeds onto each bit of paste. Leave it to dry out then plant the seed paper, covering it over with a thin layer of compost, and water gently. Your seed spacing will be ideal.

Larger seeds, including squash, can be gently pushed into the compost and covered over. While the majority of seeds can be sown directly into seed trays or direct outside from the packet, there are some hard seeds that need to be soaked or 'nicked' first to help with germination. Sweet peas and luffa seeds can be soaked first to thin the seed coat. Nasturtiums and lupins benefit from being nicked first before sowing. Use a sharp tool to make a shallow cut to the seed, which will allow water to be absorbed and provoke germination to begin.

Don't forget to label your seed trays so you can remember what you have sown. You could use lollipop sticks, reusable plant labels, or cut strips from white food containers and write on them.

Reserve a seed tin or container to store your seed packets in, even when you have used all of the seeds. You will no doubt want to look back at further instructions or even remember the name. You could file them in alphabetical order or date of sowing order.

SOWING VESSELS

Recycled pots and trays are easy to make and use, are a good way of reusing things around your home and they save you money, too.

- **Newspaper pots** can be made at home by cutting wide strips from the paper and wrapping them around a tin can. Fold in the bottom then lift the tin can out. If you need to tape the paper together (if you practise you'll find you won't need to) you can use a little brown tape. You will then be left with paper pots that you can sow seeds into that are entirely biodegradable.

- **Toilet roll cardboard centres** are perfect for seed sowing, especially for seedlings that have long roots such as sweet peas (*Lathyrus odoratus*). Save them all year and use them for sowing in spring. When the seedlings are strong enough to be planted outside, the whole cardboard roll with the seedling can be planted out and the cardboard will decompose in the soil.

- **Food containers** can also be used for seed sowing – from fruit punnets to tofu packs. Give them a good clean out, make some drainage holes in the bottom and stand them on a baking sheet or recycled tray.

- **Drink cartons** can hold compost if laid on their side with a hole cut out of the top side and drainage holes made in the bottom. Upcycle juice and milk cartons throughout the year to use whenever you need to sow seeds.

- **Drink bottles** such as soda and juice can be cut in half, and the bottom half used to sow seeds – just add drainage holes.

SOWING UNDER COVER

Sowing under cover, which could include a windowsill, conservatory, cold frame, greenhouse or plant propagator, ensures that your seeds have enough warmth and protection to germinate. It also means you can sow seeds when it is still cold outside, instead of direct sowing where they are to grow when the soil is a bit warmer. It gives your seedlings protection from slugs and snails, too. There are many seeds that you can sow under cover – always read the packet or label because both the time of year and how to sow can vary vastly between plants.

PRICKING OUT AND POTTING ON

Keep a close eye on your seedlings as they grow, and when they have at least two pairs of leaves it will be time to prick out and pot on. Pricking out means moving each seedling into a larger pot with peat-free multipurpose compost, giving it space and nutrients to grow. If you leave seedlings crowded together in a tray or pot for too long, they are more prone to a disease called 'damping off' (see page 208). At the very least, the roots will become tangled and it will be much harder to pot them on, and they could become 'leggy' (tall thin stems reaching for the light) as they try to grow. Seeds that have been individually sown or are already in trays with enough root space don't need to be pricked out.

Generally, seedlings can be potted on to 9cm (3½in) pots, but all kinds of recycled containers and modules can be used. You can use a dibber or a pencil to gently lift seedlings out, being careful not to damage the roots, or you can lift the seedling out carefully while holding the leaves and not the stem (which is very delicate at this stage). Make a hole in the compost in the larger pot, put the seedling into the hole and firm in the compost around it gently before giving it some water. Try not to rush this gardening activity as it's a delicate job, and it can be wonderfully therapeutic, too.

HARDENING OFF

As your seedlings grow, don't be in too much of a rush to get them planted out. Taking your time throughout these early stages of growth will pay off later in the season with their ultimate strength and growth. Hardening off is the process of acclimatizing young plants to the outside world so that it's not so much of a shock to them when you first plant them out. Imagine being inside, wrapped up warm, then suddenly flung outside in the freezing cold, wind, sun and rain with no clothes on – it's the same feeling for plants! Hardening off isn't just for the seedlings you have grown but also for young shop-bought plants or plug plants that have arrived in the post.

When your plants are growing, the weather is warming up and you are getting prepared to plant them outside, begin to give them exposure to the outside climate. Start by placing your seedlings outside in a sheltered place (up against a wall or in a cold frame with the top open, for example) for about an hour a day for a day or two, then for each day up to two weeks increase the exposure, always making sure to bring them back under cover at night. As long as there is no frost, strong winds or heavy rain, you can leave them in their sheltered spot overnight towards the end of the hardening off period. Your plants will now be ready for planting out wherever you want them to grow.

PLANTING OUT

When the temperature and soil has warmed up, you can start to plant out hardened-off seedlings. If you want to warm up the soil sooner, you can cover it with horticultural fleece or cloches and plant underneath (keeping them covered until it's warmer).

Plant into moist compost, firm the soil around the plants and water well. Try not to disturb the roots too much or damage the plant. As you plant out, ensure you leave ample space between plants for them to grow to their maximum size – you'll find this information on the seed packet or planting instructions.

Make sure all frosts have passed before you plant out – usually by around early May, but this can vary greatly depending on the area you live in. If you've planted out and a surprise frost is forecast, make sure you get out into the garden and cover up your young plants to protect them by using cloches or horticultural fleece.

When the weather warms up, if you don't have time to harden off plants fully, just try to give them some time outside before planting. If I am in a rush, I often lift them off the windowsill as I am leaving the house in the morning and place them in my front garden, then bring them back in when I get home from work.

DIRECT SOWING

Another method of sowing is direct into the soil where the plants will grow to maturity. This is usually done in spring (although there are some that will prefer to be sown in autumn and need the cold period to settle in). This method is helpful if you have no space inside or under cover, as you can just wait until the time is right to direct sow and the plants will soon catch up. Direct sowing or sowing under cover is part choice and part dependent on the seeds you are sowing – those seed packet instructions will tell you everything!

Make sure the area you are planting into has been weeded and there aren't any big clumps of soil or rocks. If you are unsure how deep to sow seeds, try three times as deep as the size of the seed. Water in gently, so that you don't disturb the seeds, keep moist and watch them germinate. Don't forget to label them!

THINNING OUT

You might need to 'thin out' seedlings if they are growing in rows and too close together. Thinning out is the process of removing some of the seedlings, thereby giving space to the remaining ones. You can simply thin out every other seedling or start with the weaker ones. Do this as carefully as you can to avoid disturbing the roots of the ones left in the ground to grow. Depending on what seedlings you are thinning out, you can use the thinnings in cooking so nothing goes to waste.

TOP TEN
VEGETABLE PLANTS

Growing vegetables is one of the most satisfying aspects of gardening. Growing something from a seed through to harvesting a delicious vegetable to devour is a wonderful nurturing process, through which you can learn what plants need to thrive and how food is grown. Did you know peanuts are legumes and grow underground? Did you know you can grow chickpeas in your garden and even sweet potato? There is an abundance of vegetables that can be grown, even in a small space, and all can help with a healthy diet. These are some of the easiest to get started with, all of which can be grown in containers, as well as in the ground:

1. Kale

- Sow from late spring to early summer, harvest from autumn throughout winter.
- Add organic matter to the soil before planting.
- Water in well when first planted and in dry weather.
- Protect from birds with secure netting.
- Full of vitamins A, K, B6 and C, plus minerals.

2. Garlic

- Plant cloves from autumn to winter, harvest from late spring to late summer.
- Plant in full sun and keep weeds away.
- Ensure the soil is well drained by digging in organic matter first.
- Protect from birds just as they establish.
- Full of vitamins B6 and C and minerals.

3. Beetroot

- Sow from early spring to mid-summer, harvest in summer and autumn.
- Sow successionally (sowing every two weeks to prolong harvests) in well-drained soil every two to three weeks.
- Eat a leaf or two in salads as they grow.
- Water weekly as they grow.
- Full of vitamin C, as well as fibre, folate, manganese, potassium and iron.

4. Peas

- Sow from late winter to mid-summer, harvest in summer and autumn.
- Provide support with pea sticks or canes.
- Protect with secure netting from birds.
- Water weekly as they grow.
- Full of vitamins C, E, A and B, as well as antioxidants.

5. Potatoes

- Plant in spring, harvest in summer and autumn. Plant in the ground, deep containers, old dustbins or grow bags. Store after harvest in potato sacks.
- Christmas potatoes can be planted in late summer and harvested in late autumn or early winter. Grow these outside then move inside just before the first autumn frosts.
- Water once a week as needed.
- Full of many vitamins and minerals including C and B.

6. Rhubarb

- Plant from autumn to spring, harvest in spring and summer.
- Mulch each spring. (See How to Make Compost, page 218.)
- Water during dry weather.
- Remove flower stalks when they appear, to keep the plant producing stems.
- A source of vitamins K and C, calcium and fibre.

7. Runner beans

- Sow in spring, harvest in summer and early autumn.
- Add organic matter to the soil before planting.
- Prepare canes as supports before the plants grow too big and start climbing.
- Water and harvest weekly.
- Provide vitamins A, C and K and minerals in abundance.

8. Courgettes

- Sow in spring, harvest from early summer to mid-autumn.
- Add organic matter to the soil before planting.
- Water weekly and harvest regularly.
- One plant will provide many courgettes – between 5 and 20!
- Provide a good source of vitamins C and B6, iron and calcium.

9. Radishes

- Sow from late winter to late summer, harvest all year round.
- Keep moist.
- Harvest when big enough to eat.
- Cover with mesh or fleece to protect from the flea beetle.
- High in fibre, vitamin C and folic acid.

10. Salad leaves

- Sow in spring or summer, harvest from late spring to late autumn.
- Choose 'cut and come again' varieties.
- Cut weekly and sow every two weeks.
- Keep moist.
- Good for vitamins A and C, beta-carotene and phytonutrients.

HOW TO GROW HERBS

There are herbs that can be grown in any garden or windowsill. Not only do they provide a sensory garden experience but they are also nutritious and have medicinal value. Growing herbs to harvest for a fresh cup of herbal tea or to make your own toiletries is an empowering experience, and nurturing them to full growth is both satisfying and rewarding. Culinary herbs play a vital role in a biodiverse garden, as many herb flowers will also attract beneficial insects.

Five Tips for Growing Herbs

1. You can either grow herbs from seed or buy young herbs to plant out in spring after the last frosts.
2. Most herbs will need well-drained soil in at least a partly sunny spot. The more sun the better (6 hours ideally), but make sure they aren't being totally fried!

3. Herbs rarely need feeding, although there are exceptions depending on the conditions they grow in. If you have poor soil, fast growing herbs might need some feed (see page 186). Use a gritty, well-drained compost when growing in containers.

4. Watering requirements vary greatly between herbs so always read the instructions. As a general rule, keeping the soil moderately moist will suit most herbs. Some thrive in drier conditions between watering, such as rosemary and thyme.

5. Snip herbs as and when you want to use them so you can make the most of the fresh goodness at the same time as keeping the plant in shape and stopping it from flowering too soon. Leave some to flower though and set seed, so you can collect the seeds to sow for more plants.

Supermarket herbs are not grown in conditions suitable for adapting to growing outside in your garden or even for longevity on a kitchen windowsill. Use them in cooking, try taking cuttings to root in water or remove them from the pot and the compost they are in, divide them up and re-pot to give them the best chance.

What Herbs to Grow

There are so many herbs that you could grow so, just like any plant, try to choose those that are ideal for where you want them to grow. While most like a little sun, there are even some that will grow in a shady spot.

- **Mint** is probably the herb most well-known for its medicinal value (and for mojitos!). Mint will grow in sun or part shade, and because it can take over a bed, growing it in a pot is preferable. Alternatively, sinking a pot filled with mint into a garden bed will help to contain the roots. Try lime mint, pineapple mint, chocolate mint and even strawberry mint for a taste sensation.
- **Lemon balm** is another easy-to-grow herb that grows well in shade or sun. The leaves make a refreshing herbal tea, either fresh or dried. It does take over a bed, so keep it in check by dead heading the flowers before they set seed and regularly picking some for your tea. Just like mint, it can be beneficial to stop the roots forming large clumps by keeping it in a container.
- **Sage** has a distinctive flavour and aroma, and grows well in part shade. It's so easy to grow you can plant it and almost forget it's there until you want to harvest some leaves. Sage works well in many dishes, including marinades and on focaccia.

Best Container Herbs
- **Chives** grow well in a container, producing delicate, green, onion-flavoured foliage and lilac pompom-shaped flowers that pollinators love and are also edible. Chives grow in full sun to part shade, and chopped up, they finish off a dish perfectly.

- **Salad burnet** has a crisp, cucumber flavour and complements salads and even spritzer drinks. It prefers part sun/part shade and is easy to care for, as long as it is planted in well-drained soil.
- **Lavender** is a plant for people and pollinators. Perfect for a pot, planted in well-drained compost with low watering requirements, there's no wonder it's so popular. Lavender makes a delicious ice cream.

Windowsill Herbs
- **Basil** is a must for topping off your homemade pizza and will grow well in a pot on a sunny windowsill. Basil also grows well with tomatoes and peppers as the scent may deter pests. Keeping it moist is key. You will know when it needs watering as it will start to wilt.
- **Parsley** needs sunlight, warmth and evenly moist soil. Otherwise, it's a happy plant that keeps on giving. Try curly parsley, flat leaf and Italian to see which you prefer to garnish your dishes.
- **Coriander**, or cilantro, is an annual herb that will grow in part shade. It grows fast, has a strong flavour and tops off a curry perfectly.

What, How and When to Plant

Knowing what needs to be planted and when can depend a great deal on what climate you are gardening in, but the main two planting seasons are spring and autumn. It's important to keep an eye on the weather, especially for frosts. This will, to a great extent, determine when to sow seeds, plant out and cut back. There are many plants that need the cold weather, during which they stop growing to store energy for the next burst of growth – a bit like humans sleeping at night. Other plants are like night owls and grow gloriously well over winter, feeding birds with berries, and providing homes for wildlife and a great deal of visual winter interest for us too.

An important aspect of gardening is to always look ahead and be planning for the seasons approaching. But also remember to take time to observe your plants and feel connected to the natural world around you in the present.

TREES AND SHRUBS

Ideally, trees and shrubs grown in containers should be planted out between mid-autumn and early spring, allowing them plenty of time to establish before the heat of summer. It is possible to plant out at any time of year, but during spring and summer they will require a lot more water and can be more susceptible to growth problems, if they struggle to establish due

to stress. Even though winter is the better time to plant, hold off if the ground is waterlogged or frozen. You can keep trees and shrubs in containers until the soil is easier to work.

Bare root trees (including shrubs and fruit) need to be planted as soon as you receive them because there is no soil around the root, so they will dry out quickly. If you aren't ready to plant them, they can be 'heeled in', which means creating a temporary place for them to grow:

1. Dig a trench wide enough for the roots in a sheltered position.
2. Lay the plant so the roots are in the trench and stems are at an angle/up against the edge of the trench for extra protection from bad weather.
3. Cover the roots with soil and water. (See How to Grow a Tree, page 122.)

FLOWERS

Growing flowers for your kitchen table or to gift a homegrown bouquet to friends is such a cheery thing to do! There are many annuals, perennials and bulbs that can be grown for stunning cut flowers, and most will need a bed with rich, well-drained soil in sunshine and plenty of water. Many will grow more flowers the more you cut them, so it's a win-win! What time of year you plant will depend on what you want to grow, but the majority of flowers will be in bloom from spring through to autumn, and be sown or planted in autumn or spring. Pots and containers, raised beds and garden beds are all suitable for flowers.

Annuals such as cosmos (*Cosmos bipinnatus*), godetia (*Clarkia amoena*), sunflowers (*Helianthus annuus*), zinnias (*Zinnia elegans*) and strawflowers (*Xerochrysum bracteatum*) can either be sown under cover in early spring or after the last frost; and pot marigolds (*Calendula officinalis*), love-in-a-mist (*Nigella*) and cornflowers (*Centaurea*) can be sown outside in early autumn to overwinter or/and in spring in well-drained soil and a sunny spot.

Perennials can be grown from seed, as plug plants, bare roots or as container-grown plants. When you plant each will vary, but often these are bought from a plant nursery as container-grown plants that may already be in bud or flowering. Perennials grown in containers can be planted out as soon as you have bought them, including into larger pots in your garden. Ideal times are spring and autumn, to allow them time to settle in before the hot summer. If you do plant throughout summer, keep them well watered. These might include chrysanthemums (*Chrysanthemum*), roses (*Rosa*), peonies (*Paeonia*), hydrangea (*Hydrangea*), delphiniums (*Delphinium*), cornflowers (*Centaurea*), lady's mantle (*Alchemilla*) and coneflowers (*Echinacea*).

Bulbs including spring-flowering daffodils (*Narcissus*), crocus (*Crocus*), alliums (*Allium*) and hyacinth (*Hyacinthus*) should be planted between early and mid-autumn, and tulips (*Tulipa*) in late autumn. Don't panic if you don't have time, there have been many years I haven't planted tulips until Christmas and they've still flowered perfectly the following spring. Summer-flowering bulbs such as lilies (*Lilium*) can be planted during mid- to late spring.

Corms are enlarged underground stems that are planted in the same way as bulbs. Corms such as gladioli (*Gladiolus*), crocosmias (*Crocosmia*) and freesias (*Freesia*) can be planted from mid-spring until early summer, and ranunculus (*Ranunculus*) from early spring. Corms are often grouped with tubers and rhizomes under the 'bulb' category, although each is slightly different.

Tubers are formed from a root or stem, and many shoots can grow from different places on the tuber. This group includes dahlias (*Dahlia*), which have become incredibly popular with many different varieties in all kinds of shapes and colours. Tubers are planted outside in late spring or early summer and cut back in autumn. They should be either lifted and stored in a dry place over winter or heavily mulched if left in the ground. If they are lifted, tubers need to be taken out of storage in spring and planted in pots until strong shoots have formed, before planting out again after the last frosts.

Rhizomes such as bearded irises (*Iris germanica*), cannas (*Canna*) and calla lilies (*Zantedeschia*) are similar to bulbs but they grow close to the surface of soil. Buds form on the rhizome for the following year's growth and the old rhizome will eventually need to be removed. Bearded irises can be planted in spring or autumn and will flower the following summer after planting. Cannas are best planted during mid- to late spring and will grow in well-drained soil in sun to part shade, as will calla lilies, which can be planted from early winter to mid-spring and will flower the following summer.

Wildflowers are charming, and a perfect addition to any style of garden. Attractive to pollinators and easy to grow in all size of garden, including window boxes and even in the cracks of pavements. Wildflower mixes can generally be sown in early autumn and late spring (September and May ideally). Mixes can include a number of wildflowers that can be used as cut flowers, from oxeye daisy (*Leucanthemum vulgare*) to poppies (*Papaver*) and musk mallow (*Malva moschata*).

HERBS

The majority of herbs can be grown from seed, both under cover before the soil warms up during early winter to mid-spring and outdoors when it is warmer, from early spring onwards. If you'd prefer to plant young plants (plug plants), they will need to be hardened off (see page 157) and planted out in spring. Container-grown plants can be planted most of the year but need to be kept well-watered to establish well. Herbs are easy to take cuttings from during late summer and these can be rooted in water before potting up for more free herbs (see page 164).

FRUIT BUSHES

Homemade fruit crumble, strawberry smoothies, raspberry jam and gooseberry fool can't be beaten when the fruit is harvested from your own garden. Most fruit should be planted from autumn and throughout winter from November to February. Give the roots a good soak in a bucket of water then place into a planting hole no deeper than the container and add plenty of mulch. Firm it in, water and mulch the surface, leaving a gap around the base. Some fruit will need support, so tying to a trellis can be helpful. Fruit bushes need well-drained soil and plenty of sun, although something like blueberries will tolerate some shade – just make sure they are grown in ericaceous compost (for plants that thrive in acidic soil). Blueberries are great for growing in a pot.

Plant strawberries between early to mid-autumn and early to mid-spring as dormant plants. These can be bought as bare roots, which are the cheapest option. If you have a strawberry patch already, compost old plants, as crop yields will decrease over three to four years, or divide them and replant the strongest of the divisions. When you plant, enrich the soil with some well-rotted organic matter and water in. Strawberries prefer well-drained soil in full sun but will be fine in part shade. They will grow well in pots and containers, hanging baskets, window boxes and in upcycled items such as old boots!

VEGETABLES

You'll hear it over and over again, and that's because it's true – homegrown vegetables taste the best! Delicious and organic, all the goodness comes from right outside your back door. Fresh from the garden to the kitchen, vegetables are perhaps the most satisfying plants to grow and provide us with the nutrition we need.

Legumes – peas and beans are perfect for growing in large and small spaces. Peas can be sown between late winter and mid-summer, or in autumn under cover and planted out in spring for an early crop from late spring. They need well-drained soil and plenty of sun. If it is particularly cold leading in to spring, sow peas under cover and transplant when the soil has warmed up. Runner beans and French beans can be sown under cover in late spring or directly outside in early summer, but if you have no room for sowing, you'll find plenty in plant nurseries or online. Harden the new plants off (see page 157) and plant out in early summer, after the risk of all frosts has passed. All legumes can be grown in pots and containers. Climbing beans will need tall supports and dwarf beans are ideal for pots.

Brassicas are a superfood group of plants, which includes brussels sprouts, kale, romanesco, broccoli, cabbage and cauliflower. If the correct varieties are grown in different seasons, you can harvest almost all year around. Sowing in late spring will produce a harvest from autumn throughout winter but earlier sowings will be ready to eat throughout the summer. After hardening off, late spring sowings can be transplanted in early summer. Make sure your soil has been replenished with compost so there are plenty of nutrients available, and allow that to settle before planting. When planted, firm in the soil and water at the base. Cabbage collars can be placed around the base to deter root fly.

Root vegetables include earthy parsnips and carrots, which can be used for down-to-earth, warming dishes. Sow seeds in a sunny spot from early spring through to early autumn and you'll be harvesting them almost all year. Some of the earlier varieties can be sown under cover from late winter, so check the seed packet. Root vegetables need soil that has been well prepared in autumn and allowed time to settle before sowing seeds. Clumpy or recently mulched soil can make roots appear in all kinds of shapes and sizes – they are all 100 per cent as good as big, straight roots and just as tasty, but if you are looking for a more classic shape, then well-drained, sandy soil will do the trick. If that's not possible, plant short-rooted varieties. Carrots are available in many shapes, sizes and colours. Sow parsnips direct from mid-spring to early summer or under cover a little earlier, then carefully transplant them when you see the third full leaf on the seedling.

Potatoes are super easy to grow, either in the ground or in bags, containers and old dustbins. There are varying times of the year to plant depending on the type of potato you are growing, so always check the label. If you grow some of each, you'll be harvesting potatoes from early summer through to mid-autumn. If you are growing in containers, these can be planted a little earlier than in the ground. Make sure the site is in full sun and frost free.

- **First earlies** will be planted and harvested first in early summer – plant around late March.
- **Second early**, which are a little later to harvest than first earlies – plant early to mid-April.
- **Maincrop** potatoes take the longest time to harvest from mid-summer into autumn – plant mid- to late April.

Christmas potatoes will be ready to harvest for your Christmas meal – plant in August under cover.

Onions can be grown from seed but are also very easy and cheap to grow from onion sets (young bulbs). These are mostly planted out during early to mid-spring, but some varieties can be overwintered and planted out in mid-autumn. Ensure the soil has lots of well-rotted organic matter dug in and push the sets into the soil, leaving the tips above the surface. Cover over with netting as they establish, to keep birds from pinching them.

Squash can be sown under cover from mid- to late April or direct in the ground where they will grow after the last frosts from late spring to early summer. They are readily available as plug plants online or in pots and modules from plant nurseries. They can be hardened off (see page 157) and planted out after the last frosts.

Greenhouse crops such as tomatoes, aubergines, peppers and cucamelons are generally sown from late winter to early spring to be potted on and grown under cover throughout the year. These can also be bought as plug plants or potted plants to grow in the greenhouse or outside after the last frosts.

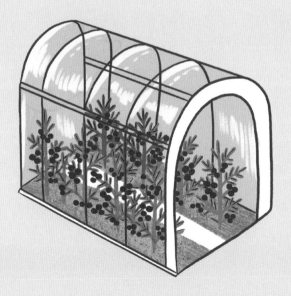

CHAPTER 5

Keeping Plants Alive

When your seeds are sprouting, your garden is full of colour and vegetables are being harvested, you will need to spend time keeping everything growing strong. From watering routines with the environment in mind and feeding with homegrown plant food, this chapter will leave you with plenty of food for thought. You'll undoubtedly come across pests and diseases when you garden, and how you deal with them will vary, but you will find no chemical solutions here. However frustrating it is to see slugs on your lettuce, nature has its own way

of creating a balanced eco-system. Just a little helping hand is required from us with environmentally friendly ways to help prevent pests or at least minimize them, and our plants will be safe. You'll find details of some of the most common garden pests in this chapter and ideas to keep them off your plants.

Diseases can take hold quickly and, therefore, prevention is mostly about spotting the signs and taking action quickly. Here, you will find easy information about good gardening practices to minimize disease, details of some of the more likely diseases you'll come across and tips of how to deal with disease if it does take hold in your garden.

Lastly, the sometimes scary-sounding prospect of pruning and dead heading is covered – neither of which should fill you with fright because generally it's just about tidying. However, if you're unsure when to take your secateurs to your plants, trees and shrubs, this guide will provide you with methods to help you tidy up and dead head plants for their good health and longevity.

Watering Your Plants

Plants need water to survive – even the most drought tolerant need water occasionally. However, we can also kill off plants in lightning speed if we water too much, especially if the plant prefers to be dry. Watering might sound tricky to navigate but it's actually very easy to work out what your plants need. Understanding what water does for plants is a good place to start.

When we water plants, the nutrients and sugar are taken up from the soil and transported through the plant with the help of water. If there isn't enough water you will notice your plants wilting; if there is too much water the roots will rot; if there is just about enough water you'll find they are hanging on in there but not at their best. Know your plants – check the label, research online, ask a plant-loving friend.

In most cases, a deep watering less often is better than a little watering regularly, but it does depend on the plant and also on your soil. A deep watering means that the water reaches deeper roots under the soil, which just a sprinkle of water will not do. Using a watering can is the best way, and using water responsibly is also important. A hose is helpful for larger areas, but be mindful of hose pipe bans in hot summer months, and use a spray attachment where possible. If you don't have a watering can, you can recycle an old drink bottle by cleaning it out, punching holes in the lid and filling with water.

HOW TO WATER CORRECTLY

Do:

- Try to water into the soil, so that it reaches deep into the ground and ultimately the roots.
- Water in the morning, where possible, when it is still cool enough for the plant roots to absorb the water before evaporation. If you have slugs and snails, it is also helpful to water in the morning. Plus, pottering in the garden with your morning cuppa is a great way to start the day – think of it as giving your plants their morning cuppa, too!
- Keep a check on the soil moisture levels. There is rarely a need to water over the winter months, but in dry warmer spells you may need to.

Don't:

- Water over the foliage, especially if you have dense planting, as the majority of the water will then sit on the plants rather than reach the roots. Leaving plants wet can also encourage diseases to spread or even burn the plant, if left sitting in hot sunshine.
- Water during the day in warm weather, as the majority of the water will evaporate instead of getting to the roots.
- Water at night if you have slugs and snails, as this is when they are most active. They will love the wet conditions and happily munch your plants. Not a sight you want to wake up to!

SOIL AND WEATHER CONSIDERATIONS

Sandy soils will not hold water as well as clay soils, which in turn might hold it too much! So, mulching your soil and improving the structure is important for soil and plant health. The no-dig method significantly helps this process. I have found limited need to water my no-dig allotment through hot, dry spells in comparison to my neighbour's plot, even though our soil is very sandy.

There is also the weather to consider. Generally, in hot, dry weather you will need to water more, while if there has been heavy rainfall, you will need to water less. However, bear in mind that some plants may be covered over by a tree canopy or sheltered, even up against a wall, meaning the rainfall might not get to them. A light rainfall won't make a huge difference at all, so you will need to continue to water.

WATERING CONTAINERS

Container plants will need more water than those in garden beds. In dry weather, watering could be needed daily. Check the soil with your hand to see how moist it is: poke your finger in and if the soil is dry, it needs to be watered. To properly water a container plant, you need to ensure the whole root ball is given a drink. Soil shrinks when it is dry, so if the container plant has dried out you will notice the soil edges have moved away from the pot leaving a small gap between the soil and side of the pot. Ideally you want to avoid this, as the plant won't benefit from the water and it is a waste. When you water at this point, a lot of what you use will simple trickle down the edges and not get to the root ball at all. In the winter months, even if the weather is cold, you don't want to leave your pots and container compost to dry out or they will struggle to come back to life in spring.

If your containers are in pot saucers, you can water into the saucer so the roots take up what they need as and when. If you water from above, do so until some water runs out of the container drainage holes or into the saucer.

Remember: the top of the soil in a garden or in a container doesn't really tell you what is going on underneath, where the roots are. If the surface is wet, that doesn't mean the roots are moist and vice versa.

GOOD ENVIRONMENTAL WATERING PRACTICES

When you have the right plants in your garden for the soil and aspect, watering needs will be less because they will be well suited to their environment. This allows you to save water and make your garden more sustainable.

Other ways to water responsibly include:

- Mulching – by far one of the best ways to retain moisture (see page 222).
- Planting mainly outside of the summer months (new plants in summer will require a lot more water to bed in).
- Water deeply, less frequently.
- Water into the soil, not over the plant foliage.
- Get a water butt and collect rainwater to use in your garden (this can also be used on houseplants).
- Choose plants that need less water and prioritize which plants need water more than others when you are watering them.

- Allow your lawn to grow longer, as this helps to retain moisture in the soil.
- Use cooled, grey water from your washing-up bowls, baths and even your laundry on non-edible plants.
- Place pots and containers under hanging baskets so that the water drips through the basket into the pots.

Drought-tolerant plants

All plants need water, although there are some that can sustain long periods of dry conditions, making them perfect for a dry garden.

- Agapanthus (African lily)
- Californian fuchsia (*Epilobium canum*)
- Mediterranean sea holly (*Eryngium bourgatii*)
- Helianthemum (rock rose)
- Ice plant (*Hylotelephium spectabile*)
- Rose campion (*Lychnis coronaria*)
- Nepeta (catmint)
- White gaura (*Oenothera lindheimeri*)
- Armenian poppy (*Papaver trinifolium*)
- Lamb's ear (*Stachys byzantina*)

Feeding Your Plants

As you will already have read in this book, I am a big fan of mulching! Unquestionably the best way to feed your plants is to feed your soil. That's where the roots take up the nutrients from, after all. Look after your soil and it will feed your plants. If you can get this balance right, there really won't be any need for further feeding.

Mulching with a well-balanced homemade compost (see page 218) is ideal, but other mulches, such as mushroom compost, are also good choices. I do not add extra feed to my garden, apart from containers with a homemade feed (see below), because mulching with a plant-based compost has always been enough for an abundance of flowers, fruit and vegetables.

FEEDING CONTAINER PLANTS

Container plants will absorb all of the nutrients in the soil quite quickly and the compost will need replenishing. Container-grown plants can only take the nutrients you supply them with, so feeding is particularly important. There are two great garden plants that are not only wonderful for wildlife, but also make up the perfect plant-based feeds.

Comfrey can be easily grown from seed. Cut back the foliage, stuff the leaves into a bucket, secure down with a brick and cover with water. In around six weeks it will be ready for you to dilute with water (one part comfrey to ten parts water) and feed your plants. Use comfrey for flowering, fruiting and vegetable plants, especially tomatoes and beans.

Nettles are likewise perfect for feeding plants. Follow the same method as with the comfrey but the feed will be ready in as little as three weeks or less. Make sure the buckets are well covered over as, quite frankly, the nettles stink! Use nettle feed for leafy salads, brassicas, fruit trees, shrubs, roses and annuals.

A WORD ABOUT FERTILIZERS

Different types of fertilizer are readily available for you to buy. Some will be pellets, some liquid and others as a mulch. Fertilizers increase plant growth, flowers and fruits, and consist of the main nutrients needed – NPK (nitrogen, phosphorus and potassium). Liquid fertilizers are generally diluted in water before application and pellets are often sprinkled around the plants then watered in. It's so important to check these are approved as organic. There are plant-based liquid feeds available along with seaweed feeds and many others. Usually you will need to apply these when the soil is moist to allow them the chance to be absorbed. Before you choose this way of gardening, consider your garden's ecosystem and the impact fertilizers could have, and whether you really do need them or if you could try plant-based feeds.

TOP TEN
EDIBLE FLOWERS

There are some surprisingly delicious and nutritious edible flowers, some of which may surprise you! The more commonly known as edible are pansies and violas, along with the many herbs and flowers used in tea such as chamomile, lavender, hibiscus and rose. However, there are edible flowers present in almost all landscapes, from the white flowers of hawthorn hedgerows to sweet apple blossom flowers. Used medicinally for centuries, flowers are also used in many cuisines around the world. When you start discovering just how many flowers are edible, it brings a whole new dynamic to gardening.

Here are my top ten flowers for incorporating into your mealtimes:

1. Gladioli (*Gladiolus*)

- Only the flowers are edible and taste similar to lettuce.
- Remove the anthers before eating.
- Sprinkle the colourful petals in salads.
- Try the flowers battered and fried.

2. Dandelion (*Taraxacum officinalis*)

- Foliage, flowers and roots are edible.
- Cook the foliage to reduce bitterness.
- Use the flowers for tea.
- Make a coffee from the roots.

3. Fuchsia (*Fuchsia* spp.)

- Flowers and berries are edible.
- Colourful flowers are peppery and sweet.
- Pop some flowers onto a salad.
- Make the berries into a jam.

4. Lilac (*Syringa vulgaris*)

- Flowers are edible but go easy, as the taste can be overpowering.
- Use as cake decorations.
- Make a lilac sugar-mix to use in baking.

5. Sunflower (*Helianthus annuus*)

- The whole sunflower head is edible.
- Toss petals into a salad.
- Petals are a little bitter, so are best mixed with other salad leaves.
- Roast the whole head and eat it like corn on the cob.

6. Pineapple sage (*Salvia elegans*)

- The flowers and leaves are edible.
- Flowers have a sweet flavour.
- Use them to garnish a dish.
- Make a pineapple sage vinegar.

7. Borage (*Borago officinalis*)

- The blue flowers are edible.
- Flowers taste similar to cucumber.
- Add them to ice cubes.
- Enjoy in a cocktail.

8. Day lily (*Hemerocallis*)

- Every part is edible.
- Flowers taste similar to asparagus.
- Harvest the unopened buds.
- Sauté the buds for a snack.

Make sure your garden edibles have been organically grown and are the correct edible plant – reference the botanical name to be sure.

9. Squash blossom/courgette flowers (*Cucurbita* cvs)

- Flowers are edible.
- Pick the flowers after pollination has occurred.
- Flowers taste a little like radish.
- Stuff with chopped vegetables and bake.

10. English Daisy (*Bellis perennis*)

- Flower buds, petals and leaves are edible.
- Open flowers can be bitter and the leaves slightly sour.
- Use the flowers as cake decorations.
- Flower buds can be pickled like capers.

How to Deal with Weeds

Weeds have a bad reputation, but undeservedly so. After all, they are simply plants that have been classified as weeds because they produce a lot of seeds, can survive a really long time hidden under the soil until disturbed, or can establish fast and spread easily. Some will grow where other more sought after plants barely stand a chance. However, there are many plants that we choose to grow with just the same ability to take over a garden if left to their own devices. A weed is just a plant growing where we don't want it to grow.

There will be weeds in every garden because seeds can blow for miles, they travel on wildlife or lay dormant in the soil just waiting for a chance to grow. Weeds are part and parcel of gardening, and weeding itself is a love or hate task. If you're not so keen, think of weeding as a wonderful way to relax and weed out your own negative thoughts or stresses of the day each time you pull a weed. When you've weeded away any unwanted plants, seeing a tidy garden bed or container is really satisfying. Don't be too hard on yourself, though, if you don't have time for weeding – your garden wildlife will enjoy a weedy patch.

TIPS FOR TACKLING WEEDS

This advice is dependent on the time and inclination you have, as well as the type of weed you are tackling, but the following tips will help in most situations:

- Pull the roots out rather than cutting across the top to completely remove weeds, otherwise many will just grow again.
- Pull perennial weeds out by hand (some can be irritating to the skin so wear gloves), including deep and creeping roots.
- Larger weeds can be easier to remove after rainfall as the soil is much softer; hoeing small, annual weeds can be easier on dry soil. By hoeing them immediately you will stop their ability to continue growing. Try not to disturb the soil too much or you could be exposing other weed seeds that you will later have to remove.
- Remove weeds before the plant sets seed so they don't spread around the garden.
- If you have a no-dig garden (see page 146), you will find less need to weed, because the mulch suppresses weed growth and blocks out the light they need to grow.

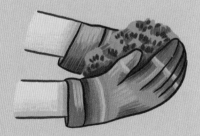

BENEFITS OF WEEDS

Just like all plants, there is a reason why each and every 'weed' grows. Many are beneficial for insects, some have medicinal properties and others are immensely nutritious. Each has a purpose, even though it may seem as if the purpose is to purely test your patience!

Perfect for pollinators – the common nettle (*Urtica dioica*) and chickweed (*Stellaria media*) are some of many weeds that are attractive to bees, butterflies and other insects. Allow some to go to flower and you will spot ladybirds and bees buzzing around your garden.

Medicinal properties – plantain (*Plantago major*) and daisies (*Bellis perennis*) are both used medicinally. Plantain to treat fevers, sore throats and bronchitis, and daisies to treat gastrointestinal issues.

Highly nutritious – dandelion (*Taraxacum officinale*) and purple/red deadnettle (*Lamium purpureum*) are not only great for pollinators but highly nutritious. Pick some to eat* and leave some for pollinators – there is no need to reach for the weedkiller as the manufacturers' adverts might suggest.

When you think about weeds in this way, you can see they are a highly underrated resource in the garden. Understandably, however, removing weeds, or at least keeping them under control, to allow space and access to nutrients for the plants you are cultivating, is high on the gardening tasks list.

Always be sure about weed identification for ingesting or topical uses, and check there are no contraindications with your medication.

TENACIOUS WEEDS

Weeds such as horsetail (*Equisetum*) and hedge bindweed (*Calystegia sepium*) can be particularly annoying. For the home gardener I cannot suggest using any herbicide, even though there are plenty to buy. Many are detrimental to the delicate ecosystem and important pollinators. As time consuming as it is, the best method to deal with these plants is to keep digging them out with as much root as you can and accept it might take some time to remove entirely. Eventually, it is possible to weaken persistent weeds enough to halt growth, and accept that you will have to partially live with it and keep on weeding. There is also the option of smothering the plant with cardboard and mulch or horticultural sheeting.

Common Pests

and How to Deal with Them in an Environmentally Friendly Way

Dealing with pests and diseases is all part of gardening. I spent many years getting upset at slugs eating my plants and red spider mite on my crops, despite cleaning my greenhouse thoroughly. Managing pests in the garden is about prevention rather than eradication. As annoying as aphids may be, they are all part of the natural world, each tiny bug playing an essential role in the ecosystem.

By far and away the best course of action to manage pests is to create a biodiverse space. Even in the smallest of gardens this can be achieved. Incorporating environmentally friendly gardening methods, such as no dig, no chemicals, ponds, planting and encouraging pollinators, will all help to create a garden to share with precious wildlife, such as birds, bats, hedgehogs and toads. In turn, pests in your garden will soon be under control naturally by beneficial predators. This way you will not be fighting pests, you will come to an understanding with them.

Sometimes you might find a plant munched, or even a whole crop destroyed. It's frustrating, but if you use chemicals and even some homemade solutions, the damage to your garden, soil and essential pollinators such as bees will be far worse.

Here are some of the common pests you might find in your garden and suggestions for how to keep them off your plants:

Aphids (black, white, green, red) – there are many aphids and most gardens will attract them. You may spot them on the stems and leaves (often the undersides) of your plants or feel a sticky sap, which is from the aphids' feeding habits. Ladybirds, lacewings and parasitic wasps all enjoy feasting on aphids (see Top Ten Plants for Wildlife, page 42). Plant companion plants such as nasturtiums (*Tropaeolum majus*) near your crops as a sacrificial plant (this means it may get eaten by the pests, while protecting your crops).

Cabbage white butterfly – this pretty white butterfly loves brassicas (sprouts, cabbage, kale) and seems to find its way on to plants no matter what you do, in an attempt to lay its eggs on the underside of leaves – quite a feat! The caterpillars can easily decimate plants. The best way to protect plants is to tightly secure butterfly netting over them. Butterfly netting has holes small enough that they can't get through but still allows access for other beneficial insects. Make sure that you secure the netting properly so that birds and other wildlife can't get stuck underneath.

Cabbage root fly – looking similar to a housefly, the larvae of this garden pest feed on cabbage roots, which will kill the plant or at the very least weaken it. They enjoy all of the brassica family, including kohlrabi and turnips. Netting is helpful to protect your plants but the holes need to be small. Alternatively, you could

place cabbage collars around the base of young plants, which will stop the flies from being able to lay eggs by the base of the plant. Thyme is also rumoured to deter them, so plant some close by.

Flea beetles – these small black beetles leave holes in the foliage of brassica plants such as radish, turnips, swede, cauliflower and more. Plants can be securely covered with a cloche or insect mesh, or you could try planting mint close by, which is said to deter them.

Pigeons and other birds – these tend to go for bulbs that have yet to establish, such as newly planted onions and unnetted peas and brassicas, which will disappear before your very eyes! Give them another food source, net over plants or try any number of deterrent, such as old CDs hanging on canes (they don't like the light reflection), bottles or cans tipped upside down on canes (they don't like the noise and movement in the wind), or even a scarecrow!

Slugs and snails – these seem to be the gardener's nemesis, and it's certainly frustrating to check a container once filled with new plants that has been completed destroyed overnight. Try copper tape around pots, rough surfaces such as grit and rough wood chip, or sprinkle the surface of your soil with an organic deterrent that they can't slide over (check your local store for options). Encourage birds with hedging and trees, bird boxes and feeders, along with frogs, toads, hedgehogs and ground beetles, as they will predate the pests and help control numbers. If all else fails, see page 202 for slug-resistant plants suggestions.

Rosemary beetle – they are harmless in small numbers but can ruin the appearance of herbs such as rosemary, thyme and lavender. I never remove them and have never had any problem, despite their perhaps unfair reputation. Birds, frogs and ground beetles will eat the larvae and often the shiny beetle itself.

Vine weevil – these insects are not a sight you want to see in the garden, especially if you are growing in containers only. They take over quickly and eat their way through the foliage while their larvae eat the plant roots. They look like a brownish/black beetle and are dreaded by the gardener! Remove weevils by hand and lift the plant out of the pot and replace the compost to ensure there are no eggs and larvae present before repotting.

There are many other pests and many other ways to manage them. Whichever method you choose, be sure to be kind and be organic – remember, we all share the same planet.

FIVE ENVIRONMENTALLY FRIENDLY
WAYS TO PREVENT PESTS

1. **Encourage healthy soil** – healthy soil means healthy plants. Ensuring your soil has a good structure with the right balance of air, water and nutrients will mean it's a host for many beneficial microbes. Plants with a strong root system are better able to deal with pests and diseases. Don't despair if you still see some pests though, as it's very natural for pests to find a home on any plant. You should find that healthy plants are able to fight them off better.

2. **Right plant, right place** – for example, plants that need water but sit in dry soil will struggle and vice versa. This can lead to the plant getting stressed, weak, diseased and smothered by pests. Providing a plant with what it needs to thrive will help it to grow strong and able to fight off pests.

3. **Companion planting** – this is a natural approach to both pest control and to increase crops by finding plants that are beneficially grown together. Scented plants are also helpful to deter pests from plants you want to keep protected. For example, I interplant French marigold (*Tagetes patula*) around my allotment and swear by them! The fragrance deters some unwanted guests at the same time as attracting beneficial insects. However, while there is a lot of anecdotal evidence to prove this, there is little scientific evidence.

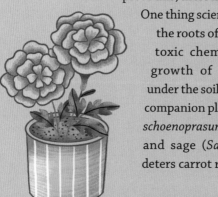

One thing scientists have proved is that the roots of French marogold emit a toxic chemical, which stops the growth of unwanted nematodes under the soil[1]. Other useful plants for companion planting are chives (*Allium schoenoprasum*), which deter aphids, and sage (*Salvia officinalis*), which deters carrot root fly.

4. **Beneficial insects** – from lacewings to ladybirds, beetles to bees and butterflies, each of these will eat the bugs you don't want in your garden. Plant with pollinators in mind – choose colourful, nectar-rich plants that not only lure bugs to your patch but also keep them there. Look for plants that have big seed heads, hollow stems and places to hide. There are many to choose from! A few of my favourites are: anise hyssop (*Agastache foeniculum*), avens (*Geum* 'Totally Tangerine') and teasel (*Dipsacus fullonum*). Some beneficial insects to attract into your garden to help encourage a biodiverse space include bees, butterflies, lacewings, beetles, hoverflies, moths, wasps, centipedes and ladybirds.

5. **Resistant plants** – some plants are either naturally or bred to be resistant to certain pests. Many will mention this on the label. Also, try asking other gardeners what their experiences are, because although science may not prove it yet, there will be many plants that seem to be avoided consistently by pests. Garlic and leeks, for example, won't be attacked by aphids.

Always be vigilant with your plants and keep a close eye on any sign of pests so that you can take the necessary action.

TOP TEN
SLUG-RESISTANT PLANTS

No matter what you plant there are bound to be hungry snails and slugs in your garden. It is true that often they head for diseased or damaged plants, but don't be mistaken in thinking that's all they will eat. If they are particularly attracted to a plant, it doesn't matter how perfect it is growing, you'll soon find it munched up. Typically, they do like young shoots, so take protection seriously when planting out. The good news is that there are some plants that slugs and snails just don't like, which could be down to toxic leaves, or even too much hair or texture:

1. Lady's mantle (*Alchemilla Mollis*)

- Frothy lime green/yellow flowers in summer.
- Plant in sun or part shade in any soil type.
- Will freely self-seed.
- Great for cut flower foliage.

2. Japanese anemone (*Anemone hupehensis*)

- Perennial pink or white flowering plant for late summer/autumn.
- Plant in part shade and well-drained soil.
- Will grow in full sun but keep moist.
- Flowers stand tall on stems up to 150cm (60in).

3. Chinese silver grass (*Miscanthus sinensis*)

- Easy to grow and very low maintenance.
- Grow in full sun or part shade.
- Various colours depending on the variety.
- Provides texture and movement.

4. Fleabane (*Erigeron*)

- Perennial plant growing to about 25cm (10in) tall.
- Daisy blooms that flower for a long period throughout summer.
- Plant in full sun and well-drained soil.
- Will tolerate dry conditions.

5. Stonecrop sedum (*Hylotelephium spectabile*)

- Fleshy succulent with showy pink flowers in autumn.
- A magnet for bees.
- Will grow in dry conditions.
- Plant in full sun with well-drained soil.

6. Columbine (*Aquilegia*)

- Pretty perennial with many colourful varieties.
- Easy to grow, freely self-seeding.
- Plant in sun to part shade.
- Ideal for cottage gardens.

7. Spurge (*Euphorbia*)

- Striking perennial in mostly green tones.
- Plant in sun but some will grow in shade.
- Not particularly fussy about soil type.
- Toxic sap, so wear gloves when handling.

8. Lamb's ear (*Stachys byzantina*)

- Perennial with soft, fuzzy leaves.
- Plant in full sun to part shade.
- Will grow in dry to moderately moist soil.
- Great for the front of borders.

9. Foxglove (*Digitalis*)

- Biennial or perennial.
- Moist, well-drained soil.
- Will grow in full sun to full shade.
- Let them self-seed for more plants.

10. Beggarticks (*Bidens ferulifolia*)

- Short-lived perennials grown as annuals.
- Yellow flowers on stems up to 30cm (12in) tall.
- Needs full sun and well-drained soil.
- Will grow in dry conditions.

Common Plant Diseases and Their Remedies

You will undoubtedly discover diseased plants in your garden throughout the year. It is not necessarily a reflection of your gardening skills, although there are good practice guidelines to implement to ensure diseases are limited, at least. There are so many factors that contribute to disease, from stressed plants to climatic changes, and many others in between. A biodiverse and balanced garden is the best way to prevent diseases, and if something does come along (many diseases are airborne, travel in soil, on newly bought infected plants, for example), your plants will be better equipped to cope with them.

WHAT DO DISEASES LOOK LIKE?

Diseases show up in numerous ways, from black spots or powdery blotches to distorted leaves and soggy flower heads. When you know what your plants should look like when healthy, you can quickly see any changes that shouldn't be there or look different to the norm. Distorted or stunted growth, raised orange blemishes or rotten fruit can all be signs of a disease taking hold. Keep an eye on your plants when you water and dead head as often as you can, so that you can take quick action if you do see a disease in your garden.

GOOD PRACTICE TO LIMIT
THE SPREAD OF DISEASES

- Always ensure you have healthy, well-drained soil with lots of organic matter full of nutrients to keep your plants as strong and healthy as possible.
- Check all plants before you purchase for signs of pests and diseases, and all delivered plants before you plant them outside.
- Plant disease-resistant varieties, if possible (this will be noted on the seed packet or label).
- Learn which diseases are more likely to affect your plants specifically, so that you know what to look out for.
- Ensure there is good air circulation around your plants by planting at the correct spacing, removing dead, diseased and damaged material, and providing ventilation for under-cover plants.
- Dig out larger weeds around your plants to create more space.
- When growing vegetables, it can be helpful to practise crop rotation (not growing the same crops in the same place every year).
- Keep your garden tools clean. Wash them with hot, soapy water after use, especially if you've been using them around plants with diseases. It's up to you how often to wash them. I tend to do this seasonally, unless used on diseased material or around pests.
- Water in the morning and directly into the soil rather than over plant foliage, to avoid leaving moisture on the leaves.

COMMON DISEASES TO LOOK OUT FOR

You might find any of the following diseases affecting the plants in your garden:

Brown rot can show up on fruit such as apples, pears, cherries and other ornamental trees. You'll see rotting fruits and creamy/white pimples on the skin. Prevention is better than cure in most cases of disease, so always follow planting and care instructions to keep your trees thriving and strong. Even so, the infection can enter via insect damage or splits on the fruit for any number of reasons. Remove brown rotten fruit, which is inedible when infected, and any dead twigs or other material. Many fruits will fall to the ground, which should also be discarded along with the leaves.

Apple and pear scab causes brown spots on fruits and blotches on leaves, as well as cracks on stems that can subsequently allow canker to take hold. Early or light stages of the disease doesn't affect the ability to eat the fruits, but as they get worse and crack, the fruits won't store for long and will rot.

Club root is an infection of brassica roots that will make the plant look distorted and swollen. The disease can kill the infected plants and result in reduced crops, at the very least. Without being able to see the roots, you will notice plants wilting and not growing very well. Remove the entire root system and practise crop rotation, wash your tools and replenish the soil with well-rotted organic matter.

Damping off is something you might see after sowing seedlings – it's caused by pathogens in soil and will kill affected seedlings. They look like they are withering away or collapsing at a pace, and it favours wet and cold soil. Always sow into clean pots and trays with seed compost (not garden soil). Don't overwater, and provide your seedlings with the correct heat and light as per the packet instructions. If damping off happens, discard the seedlings and the compost and start afresh.

Downy mildew causes green or brownish patches on the top of foliage, and grey or white patches under the leaf. Improve air circulation around plants, removing weeds and overcrowded plants. Prune out diseased foliage but if the plant is badly infected, you may need to remove the whole plant. There are some mildew-resistant plant varieties, so if you find plants are susceptible in your garden, look out for the relevant varieties next time.

Grey mould is very common and hits soft fruits and under-cover crops. It affects plants in high humidity, stressed plants, non-stressed plants or wounded plants. Fuzzy, grey mould is the telltale sign, but on some plants the stems will die off without signs of the mould. Remove dead and diseased material, keep greenhouses and structures clean and give plants that are under cover plenty of ventilation.

Onion white rot can be seen at the base of allium plants including onions, garlic and leeks. It remains in the soil for many years, so practising crop rotation can help, if you have enough space. The foliage may wilt and appear like it is yellowing. At the base there will be white, fuzzy mould and the plants may even feel loose in the soil. If the disease hasn't progressed too much, crops are still edible but won't store, so need to be eaten straight away. As with most diseases, replenish the soil, ensure good air circulation, don't overwater and wash tools if used in infected soil.

Potato and tomato blight are extremely common – brown/black patches can be seen on the foliage and eventually the stems, until the plants wilt and die. It's an airborne disease, so there is little you can do apart from remove infected foliage as soon as you see it, in order to keep the plant and crops growing for as long as possible. When you remove the plants, take them to the green waste at your local recycling centre and don't compost them, as the disease can still spread. Potato tubers can be left in the ground after you've cut back the diseased foliage but will still need to be harvested and eaten as soon as possible.

Powdery mildew is a grey or white dust on the foliage of many plants and can stunt growth, but pruning out diseased material can help to stop the spread. Plants should always be grown at the correct distance apart for good airflow, and try to water into the soil and not over foliage, which leaves moisture on the leaves and provides the ideal environment for mildew to grow.

Rust affects many different garden plants and initially shows up as orange (or yellow/brown) spots on foliage that may also appear raised. The plant might not thrive or, if severely infected, it could die. If you catch it early on and only a few leaves are infected, just prune them off, but otherwise remove the rust-infected parts of the plant after flowering and don't compost them.

Avoid composting diseased material to ensure the risk of spreading disease is kept to a minimum. Dispose of diseased plants in the rubbish or take them to your local recycling centre, where they can go into the green waste bins and be heat-treated to kill off the spores. If you use any sprays or other treatments for diseases, always choose options that are friendly to the planet and everything that lives on it.

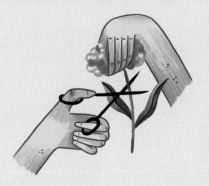

Dead Heading and Pruning

These two important tasks can make a big difference to your garden. Both dead heading and pruning will help plants to thrive. Knowing if, what, when and where to prune or dead head is another reason to keep plant labels, as many will include this in the instructions, and if not, you can research what needs to be done for each plant when you want to.

DEAD HEADING

Dead heading is a love or hate task in the garden, and I love it very much! It's quite therapeutic and very easy, with the outcome being more flowers – so that's got to make the time spent well worth it. This is one task to keep on top of, in order to keep plants that need dead heading flowering on and on and looking their best. It doesn't take long and is important to promote new growth. Dead heading is for plants in beds, pots, containers and hanging baskets, keeping them looking fresh for as long as possible. There is no need to dead head everything though, especially plants that produce seed heads for wildlife. Many can be left, and look spectacular even when the colour has faded. Others will happily self-seed, meaning you won't have to sow seeds again because they will germinate the following year where they have fallen.

HOW TO DEAD HEAD

You can simply use your fingers and thumbs to nip below the base of the flower and pull it off, but some tougher stems will need a sharp snip with secateurs or scissors. Remember to pop everything you've snipped off into the compost bin. Dead head as and when needed as the flowers fade, and after a good session, water and feed your plants to give them all the help they need to continue blooming.

Common plants that respond well to dead heading include:

- Sweet pea (*Lathyrus odoratus*)
- Zinnia (*Zinnia elegans*)
- Petunia
- Marigold (*Tagetes*)
- Roses (*Rosa*)
- Yarrow (*Achillea millefolium*)
- Balloon flower (*Platycodon grandiflorus*)
- Blanket flower (*Gaillardia*)
- Cornflower (*Centaurea*)

SEED SAVING

It's worth noting that many flowers will eventually set seed, meaning you can save some of these seeds for sowing again. I tend to dead head until the last of the flowers at the end of the season, then allow the ones I want to sow again to set seed so I can collect a packet. Some I leave for wildlife to enjoy and others I snip off for saving. This means you won't have to purchase again and you have what you want to grow if they aren't available. It's also a thoughtful gardening practice, teaching you to appreciate that seeds should not be treated as an endless resource. Seed saving is a terrifically empowering habit, as it helps you to become more self-sustainable.

Easy flowers to collect seeds from or to allow self-seeding include:

- Cosmea (*Cosmos bipinnatus*)
- Love-in-a-mist (*Nigella damascena*)
- Sunflower (*Helianthus*)
- Marigold (*Tagetes*)
- Pot marigold (*Calendula officinalis*)
- Forget-me-not (*Myosotis sylvatica*)
- Hollyhock (*Alcea rosea*)
- Foxglove (*Digitalis*)
- Columbine (*Aquilegia*)
- Snapdragon (*Antirrhinum majus*)

PRUNING

Pruning encourages healthy growth, which we all want for our plants. It is a method of ensuring your plants thrive and grow into the shape and size that you choose. Pruning helps airflow through the plant and will ensure the plant stays healthy. There are also plants that need pruning after flowering has finished, to help promote more flowering and fruit the following year. Another reason for pruning is to remove dead, diseased and damaged plant material, which will keep the plant healthy and minimize pests and diseases.

Pruning can seem complex at first, as there are various pruning methods used for different plants and outcomes. Ultimately, if you have plants, shrubs or trees that look messy or overgrown, they need pruning, and keeping on top of it makes the task much easier and less time-consuming overall.

Here are some standard pruning methods to follow:

Perennial Chelsea chop – named after the RHS Chelsea Flower Show, this is a method to prune back some summer-flowering plants. Cutting back growth by one third to keep the plant more compact and to delay flowering until later in the season, or cutting half of the stems back, will extend the flowering season. If it's a dry season, I wouldn't recommend this as it would be too much stress for your plants, and some woody plants won't thank you for it either. Personally, at this time of year I have enough to do and this just isn't on my agenda. I prefer to let them grow just as and when they should.

Formative pruning and trimming – pruning hedges is generally 'formative' in the early years, then becomes 'trimming' to shape thereafter. Formative is about creating the shape of the shrub or tree, while trimming is about keeping it in that shape. It's important to only prune or trim when there are no nesting birds. The times of year to do this are easy to remember: for evergreens, undertake formative pruning during springtime for two years after planting and any light trimming can be done in the summer; for deciduous hedging, get stuck into the light trimming in the summer and formative pruning for two years after planting during the winter months. After the first two years, the hedge should be structured in the shape you would like it to be, so the trimming is just to maintain it.

Removing damage or disease – evergreen trees need very little pruning, but dead, diseased and damaged parts should always be removed. For deciduous trees, this can be done from autumn and throughout winter, when nesting is not taking place and when the trees are dormant, before new growth starts when the weather gets warmer. For large trees, or if you are unsure and if there is a tree preservation order in place, it is best to consult an expert.

Pruning flowering shrubs – the timing of this process depends on when it flowers and if the flowers are on growth from new or old wood. If the shrub has flowers on new wood each year, these can be pruned in winter to early spring, giving them enough time to grow in time for summer flowering again. If flowering is on old wood (on stems from the previous year), they need to be pruned after the flowers have faded. If you leave this too late, it may impact negatively on the amount of flowers for the following year.

Common trees and shrubs that need pruning include:

Apple and pear trees should be pruned during the dormant season from November to March, using sharp, clean tools. Stand back and look at the shape of the tree – you are aiming for good airflow and a goblet shape. Remove crossing branches and inward-growing shoots, and cut back the previous year's growth to approximately one third. Cut above a bud and make sure it is facing the way you would like it to grow, as this will later minimize the need for pruning crossing branches again. This all sounds like a lot of work! But once you get started, you will soon see what needs doing and know that you are helping your tree to live its best life.

Forsythia needs very little pruning when young. As it grows, prune after flowering during mid-spring each year. Remove any dead, diseased or damaged growth, as well as anything overcrowded throughout the centre of the shrub, then cut about one third of the older branches low down to the ground. If you have a particularly old shrub, you can prune it right back to about 10cm (4in) from the ground and trim it gently for a year or two until it grows into its former glory.

Buddleja (Butterfly bush) needs to be pruned hard to keep it under control, in a good shape and to produce lots of flowers for butterflies. Prune as it is coming into growth in early spring. Prune back at least half of the growth from the top, then work around from the bottom removing all dead, diseased, damaged and crossed-over stems. It'll then be much easier to cut back the larger stems that might need loppers to do the job. Cut back to 60cm (24in) for a taller shrub or around 30cm (12in) for something a bit more compact. Make sure to prune just above new buds, if possible. My buddleja gets a ruthless chop each spring and continues to burst into bushy growth.

Hydrangea pruning or dead heading depends on which variety you are growing. The flower heads look magical in winter and great in dried flower displays, so don't be too quick with your secateurs. Here is some advice for the most popular:

- Mopheads (*Hydrangea macrophylla*) only need light pruning in late spring. Simply dead head the old flowers and remove dead, diseased or damaged stems. On older mopheads, it can be helpful to cut back a few stems to ground level, as this will encourage fresh, new growth.
- Lacecap (*Hydrangea macrophylla*) can be dead headed in autumn or spring, but leaving the flower heads on over winter

gives lovely garden interest for you and wildlife. Snip them back to a pair of buds below the flower head and continue the same as you would for mopheads.

- Paniculate (*Hydrangea paniculata*) and smooth (*Hydrangea arborescens*) need around one third of the stems cut back low and above a pair of buds. Then remove all dead, diseased or damaged material.

Perennials are perhaps the easiest to prune. You can choose to cut back in autumn or spring. In autumn, pruning them down to ground level leaves the garden tidy, but it also means there is no interest throughout winter and less food and shelter for wildlife. You can, therefore, leave perennials until spring and as new growth emerges, cut back the old stems close to the ground. Earlier flowering perennials, such as delphiniums, can be cut back after flowering in early summer – you might find them flowering again, which is such a pleasure. If you do leave them over autumn, there's no harm in snipping a few stems, hanging them to dry and using them in dried flower arrangements.

PRUNING LIKE A PRO

- After pruning any tree, shrub or plant, give it a good water and mulch. This will help to retain the moisture and give the plant an extra boost into strong growth.
- When you are pruning larger shrubs and trees, lay a sheet down underneath, making it easier to collect up the clippings. Use larger, woody branches to make a pile of wood for insects, smaller stems and twigs in an insect hotel, and put the rest on the compost pile.
- I recommend reading the RHS pruning group information on their website for further details.[2]

HOW TO MAKE COMPOST

Garden compost is a nutrient-rich, natural soil replenisher that you can make in your own garden from waste matter. It's not for sowing seeds or potting plants directly into but is perfect for adding plant-based nutrients into your soil at the same time as reducing waste.

Compost is exceptionally satisfying to make, and spreading your homemade compost on your garden to feed the soil for your plants to thrive is a rewarding feeling. Not forgetting it's also entirely free and saves buying heavy bags of compost and lugging them home. Composting can be fun and fruitful; turning what we consider to be waste into a valuable resource is good for

the planet. The decaying matter goes back into the cycle of gardening life and will eventually go towards feeding more plants.

You can build your own compost bin from pallets or buy a wooden bin with slats at the front to keep the contents from spilling out into your garden. There are also neat plastic bins and even 'hot bins' that speed up the compost-making process by heating the contents faster than in a garden compost-pile can.

Turning the Compost

As plants decompose in your compost bin you will need to turn the compost so that the heated, decomposed material in the middle gets some oxygen. The action of turning the compost allows microbes to breathe. If there is no oxygen, they will die off and the compost heap will take longer to decompose. Turn the compost every few weeks with a garden fork, and your homemade organic matter should be ready from three months to two years, depending on the balance and size of the compost pile. It is worth the wait. If you don't have time to turn it, compost will still decompose, it will just take a lot longer.

What About Weeds?

Some will tell you not to compost weeds, neither young weeds nor rooted weeds; others will tell you to put them all – even the most tenacious – into the compost pile. As a compromise between those opposing approaches, I compost young weeds and weeds that haven't gone to seed.

THINGS TO COMPOST

To make a well-balanced compost including green waste (nitrogen-rich) and brown waste (carbon-rich), you can throw all of the following in the compost pile:

- Uncooked vegetable scraps and peelings
- Teabags (ideally without the bag, which may contain plastic)
- Coffee grounds
- Soft and woody prunings
- Cardboard/newspaper
- Waste paper
- Grass cuttings
- Bedding from pets (hat/straw/wood shavings)
- Twigs
- Old plants
- Leaves
- Younger weeds
- Wood ash in moderation

Things NOT to Compost

Many of the following will increase unwanted garden visitors such as rats, some won't break down, worms can't eat them and overall they will make your compost bin stink!

- Meat
- Dairy
- Fats
- Oils
- Pet poop
- Charcoal ash (this leaves an unhealthy residue that is harmful to plants)

Leaf Mulch

When leaves fall from trees, it's nature's own way of replenishing the soil. It can seem such a chore to rake them up but if you do, store them in leaf bags or just as a pile with air but no water – they will become the most wonderful, natural plant mulch. Place the leaves in a sheltered spot and they will rot down in no time at all. The resulting leaf mulch created the following year is great for conditioning the soil around the base of plants (leave a gap between the mulch and the base) – it will suppress weeds, keep the temperature constant, add nutrients and help to retain moisture. Over time, using this approach can improve your soil substantially. Leaves contain a large percentage of the nutrients that tree roots absorb from the earth, so it makes perfect sense that when they fall, they are replenishing the earth all over again.

*Ideally you are looking for a **50/50 balance of green and brown waste.** If you were to only put grass clippings and leaves in your bin, for example, the resulting compost wouldn't be very good at all. So, a mixture of materials is better than a lot of just one or two.*

The Gardening Year at a Glance

The seasons can have blurred lines, and the transitions between each of them can vary greatly depending on your location. Some plants will bloom in summer and long into autumn. This guide to the gardening year is not exhaustive, but will give you a general idea of what can be done each season. There is always more to sow and grow when gardening!

SPRING

One of the busiest times of the year for a gardener is during the spring. As the bulbs start popping up through the soil and sunnier days approach, it's time to kick off the growing season once again. There's no rush, even though it may feel like it, but the flurry of activity in the garden is really quite exciting. With more daylight, you'll spot increased wildlife activity and trees beginning to blossom. Enjoy every moment, doing the tasks you can with the time you have. Don't worry about what you don't have time for, what doesn't get done can go on your list for next year.

What's Flowering

Daffodil, crocus, hyacinth, allium, iris, lilac, fruit tree blossom, camellia, grape hyacinth, magnolia, peony, bluebell, forget-me-not, primrose, violet, wallflower, rhododendron, azalea, lungwort and pasque flower.

What to Sow

Lettuce, tomato, salads, turnip, beetroot, cauliflower, herbs, peas, carrot, summer and autumn cabbage, leek, spinach, spring onion, kohlrabi, broad bean, runner bean, brussels sprout, parsnip, wildflower mix, sunflower, nigella, godetia, zinnia, cosmos and microgreens.

KEY TASKS TO TACKLE

- Sow vegetables, cut flowers and annuals (see page 152).
- Harden off young seedlings (see page 157).
- Plant out summer-flowering bulbs (see page 158).
- Clean pots, tools, cloches, bird feeders and furniture.
- Add some mulch to your garden beds if you didn't in autumn (see page 186).
- Get on top of weeding as soon as needed (see page 192).
- Water pots and containers during warmer weather.
- Lift, divide and replant perennials for more plants.
- Mow the lawn on a high setting when the weather warms up.
- Sow lawn seed to reinvigorate bare patches.
- Dead head winter pansies to encourage more flowers (see page 211).
- Dead head faded spring bulbs but leave the foliage until it dies back.
- Add fresh compost to pots, containers and raised beds.
- Create new garden beds (see page 146).
- Make a wildlife pond (see page 93).

What to Harvest

Rhubarb, sprout, kale, broccoli, parsnip, leek, salads, swede, chicory, celeriac, asparagus, oriental leaves and radish.

SUMMER

Sunny long days are perfect for pottering in the garden, and the excitement will build as your plants start flowering and fruiting. If you grow fruit and vegetables, the harvests will be in full gear at this point, so schedule in time for preserving, storing and cooking, too. Keeping everything thriving throughout summer is the main task, and don't forget to give yourself a pat on the back for what you have achieved so far.

What's Flowering

Dahlia, marigold, zinnia, sunflower, echinacea, lavender, poppy, yarrow, hydrangea, rose, phlox, daylily, gladiolus, foxglove, petunia, begonia, clematis, honeysuckle, oxeye daisy, tick seed, delphinium, geranium, gerbera, iris, lily, salvia, fuchsia, hosta, buddleja, potentilla, spirea, herbs, pieris, cistus, hebe and scabious.

What to Sow

Radish, onion, salad leaves, turnip, swede, carrot, cucumber, spring onion, runner bean, kale, herbs, fennel, beetroot, peas, pak choi, endive, chicory, brussels sprout, cabbage, cauliflower and microgreens.

What to Harvest

Broad bean, runner bean, French bean, strawberry, salads, tomato, carrot, cherry, raspberry, gooseberry, potato, herbs, radish, kohlrabi, aubergine, beetroot, chilli, pepper, chicory, courgette, cucumber, blackberry, garlic, globe artichoke, celery, spinach, onion, peas, plum, shallot, turnip, red/white and blackcurrants, apple, apricot, melon, pak choi, broccoli, fig and sweetcorn.

KEY TASKS TO TACKLE

- Successional sow for more crops throughout summer (see page 152).
- Keep on top of weeding so plants aren't competing for nutrients.
- Water and feed, especially containers, hanging baskets and raised beds (see page 180).
- Prune herbs before flowering to give them a second burst.
- Earth up potatoes to make sure they are not exposed to light. (Earthing up involves mounding up the soil around the foliage as it grows.)
- Pinch out tomato side shoots so the energy is directed towards the fruits.
- Keep dead heading to prolong flowering (see page 211).
- Prune spring-flowering deciduous shrubs.
- Top up bird baths and ponds with water as needed.
- Water evergreen shrubs, even if they are not flowering.
- Prune out dead, diseased or damaged material.
- Trim hedges when bird nesting has finished.
- Harvest fruit, vegetables and cut flowers as often as you can.
- Keep an eye out for pests and diseases (see page 196).
- Turn the compost pile (see page 218).

AUTUMN

As the leaves turn and summer flowering plants die off, it's time for the big garden tidy up. Don't forget that messy areas are essential homes for wildlife, so leaving a pile of leaves, wood and seed heads is beneficial for biodiversity and means you'll have less to do. Autumn harvests, from pumpkins to kale, are some of the most satisfying, and as the days shorten, it's the season to get planning for spring.

What's Flowering

Rudbeckia, aster, chrysthanthemum, snapdragon, helenium, sedum, crocosmia, red hot poker, delosperma, penstemon, colchicum, nerine, hesperantha, anemone.

What to Sow

Wildflower mixes, microgreens, broad bean, hardy peas, spinach, spring onion, hardy oriental leaves, salads, carrot, sweet pea, calendula, lupin, nigella, cerinthe, larkspur, poppy and mizuna.

What to Harvest

Pumpkin, butternut squash, kale, cabbage, cauliflower, brussels sprout, apple, cape gooseberry, cranberry, sweet potato, salads, grapes, leek, swede, celeriac and mizuna.

KEY TASKS TO TACKLE

- Plant out spring flowering bulbs (see page 158).
- Finish weeding (see page 192).
- Mulch beds and borders.
- Clear away old plants.
- Add frost protection for salads such as horticultural fleece, cloches or putting them in a greenhouse.
- Net remaining brassicas to protect from birds.
- Cut back perennials but also leave some for wildlife.
- Plant onions, shallots and garlic.
- Pot some herbs for the kitchen windowsill throughout winter (see page 164).
- Rake up leaves and make leaf mulch (see page 221).
- Move tender plants under cover to protect from frost.
- Make sure structures are secure for winter.
- Move pots and containers onto pot feet to improve drainage.
- Replenish hanging baskets, pots and containers with winter bedding plants.
- Stop mowing the lawn and give the mower a clean.

WINTER

The colder days of winter give us and the garden time to rest and store energy for the months ahead. While there is less to do in the garden, there are still winter jobs to take care of, so wrap up warm and get outside when you can. Winter harvests are simply delicious! If you'd rather stay indoors, put your feet up and plan what you would like to do in the garden for the following year and have a read of seed catalogues and gardening books. There are seeds that can be sown under cover by February but there is absolutely no need, unless you can't wait!

What's Flowering

Christmas box, gorse, heather, pansy, viola, snowdrop, winter aconite, daphne, mahonia, winter-flowering clematis, goldenrod, Christmas rose, cyclamen, witch hazel, viburnum, skimmia, cornus, mahonia and wintersweet.

What to Sow

Broad bean, onion, leek, peas, sweet pea, globe artichoke, spinach, salad leaves, tomato, brussels sprout and sprouting broccoli.

What to Harvest

Brussels sprout, cauliflower, kale, leek, parsnip, celeriac, cabbage, swede, endive, pak choi, turnip, chard and mizuna.

KEY TASKS TO TACKLE

- Prune apple and pear trees (see page 213).
- Clean your greenhouse, cold frames or other structures.
- Chit first early potatoes on a warm windowsill towards spring. (Chitting is placing your seed potatoes with the 'eyes' facing upwards, allowing them to shoot before planting.)
- Make time for planning the following year in the garden.
- Top up bird feeders regularly.
- Cut back ornamental grasses.
- Prune blackcurrants, gooseberries and redcurrants.
- Force rhubarb plants by covering with a bucket or pot to exclude light.
- Brush heavy snow off branches to ensure they don't snap under the weight.
- Gently break frozen pond water to allow wildlife to get in and out.
- Break down your Christmas tree to use the branches as pea supports.
- If you've lifted dahlia tubers, remove any that have signs of rot.
- Limit walking on a frozen lawn, to protect it in bad weather.
- Trim deciduous hedges before the nesting season begins (see page 214).

Glossary

Acidic – soil that is below pH 7.

Aeration – allowing air to get to the soil.

Alkaline – the majority of garden soil is alkaline (above pH 7).

Annual – a plant that grows, flowers and seeds all in one season only.

Bare root – a plant sold without soil around the roots and usually planted during winter.

Bedding plants – used to make a temporary display and are usually annuals.

Biennial – the plant's growth begins in the first year and finishes in the second year, when it flowers and seeds.

Compost – decomposed living material that is soil-like and full of nutrients.

Dappled shade – similar to partial shade but often referred to in woodland, or if plants are under deciduous trees.

Dead heading – removing faded flower or seed heads from a plant.

Deciduous – trees and shrubs that drop their leaves over winter.

Deep shade – generally no sun at all.

Direct sow – seeds sown in the place you would like them to grow and mature.

Divide/split – a method of plant propagation where the plant is split into two through the roots, allowing more room for developing roots and creating another plant for growing.

Dormancy – the time of year when the plant is storing energy below the soil for growth when the weather warms up.

Established – a plant that has settled into its home with a strong root system.

Evergreen – trees and shrubs that remain in leaf all year round.

Filler – plants used to fill the middle of a container that complement the other plants around them.

Full shade – less than four hours of sun per day.

Full sun – six or more hours of full sun a day.

Fungicide – a type of pesticide that kills fungal disease.

Germination – when a seed starts to sprout.

Half hardy – plants that will survive the cold but not a heavy frost.

Harden off – when a plant is gradually acclimatized to cooler temperatures before planting out permanently.

Hardy – plants that will live through the cold winter period.

Herbaceous perennial – plants that die down over winter to the ground and grow again the following spring.

Herbicide – a type of pesticide that

kills plants and often other wildlife.

Humus – the organic matter in soil that provides nutrients and provides the soil with the ability to retain moisture.

Micro climate – an area in a garden with a different climate from the general environment around it.

Mulch – material such as bark or compost, used to retain moisture in the soil, smother weeds and protect plant roots.

No dig – a method of gardening where the soil structure is retained by not digging it at all.

Organic – all-natural, sustainable and environmentally friendly gardening, without the use of chemicals.

Overwintering – plants that grow over winter both inside or outside.

Part sun/part shade – in direct sun for four to six hours per day.

Peat free – compost that has not had peat added to it for environmental reasons.

Perennial – plants that will grow again every spring.

Pesticide – chemicals targeted to kill certain pests.

Plug plant – germinated seedlings grown in a small cell with good root development.

Pruning – shaping, improving structure and growth of a plant.

Root bound – when a plant's roots fill out the root ball and have nowhere else to go.

Scorch – if a plant has yellow/brown leaves due to too much sun or pesticide use.

Seedlings – very young plant grown from seed.

Self-seed – where the seeds have been produced and spread to the soil to grow.

Spiller – plants used at the edges of containers to trail or spill out of the pot.

Thinning out – a method of removing weaker seedlings, allowing more room for the remaining ones to grow.

Thriller – plants in the centre or back of a container that add height and drama.

Tilth – the health of soil. Good soil with a balance of water, air and nutrients is described as good tilth.

Top dressing – spreading a new layer of soil on top of existing soil to provide more nutrients.

Topsoil – the precious upper layer of soil.

Transplanting – moving a plant from one growing medium to another.

Variegated – where any part of the plant has different colours.

Veganic – organic gardening without the use of any animal products.

End Notes

CHAPTER 1: THE BASICS
Botany Basics
[1] https://www.ncbi.nlm.nih.gov/pmc/articles/PMC5912204/

Plant Names Demystified
[2] https://arboretumfoundation.org/2016/04/10/say-what-pronouncing-botanical-latin/

Why Garden?
[3] https://www.sciencedirect.com/science/article/pii/S0264275121000160#:~:text=Significant%20associations%20were%20found%20between,with%20greatest%20perceived%20health%20benefits.

CHAPTER 2: UNDERSTANDING YOUR SPACE
Get to Know Your Soil
[1] https://www.colorado.edu/today/2017/01/05/study-linking-beneficial-bacteria-mental-health-makes-top-10-list-brain-research

CHAPTER 4: PLANTING INTO SOIL
How to Make a New Garden Bed
[1] https://eprints.whiterose.ac.uk/171212/6/1-s2.0-S0264275121000160-main.pdf

CHAPTER 5: KEEPING PLANTS ALIVE
Common Pests and How to Deal With Them in an Environmentally Friendly Way
[1] http://faculty.ucr.edu/~atploeg/PDF%20PAPERS/PLANT%20DISEASE/PLANTDISEASE.pdf

Deadheading and Pruning
[2] https://www.rhs.org.uk/pruning/rhs-pruning-groups

Further Reading

BOOKS

Dowding, Charles & Hafferty, Stephanie, *No Dig Organic Home & Garden: Grow, Cook, Use & Store Your Harvest* (Permanent Publications, 2017)

Lawson, Nancy, *The Humane Gardener: Nurturing a Backyard Habitat for Wildlife* (Princeton Architectural Press, 2017)

Richards, Huw, *Veg in One Bed: How to Grow an Abundance of Food in One Raised Bed, Month by Month* (DK, 2019)

Stuart-Smith, Sue, *The Well Gardened Mind: Rediscovering Nature in the Modern World* (William Collins, 2021)

The Royal Horticultural Society, *How to Garden When You're New to Gardening* (DK, 2018)

Thomas, Ceri, *Gardeners' World, 101 Ideas for Pots: Foolproof Recipes for Year-Round Colour* (BBC Books, 2007)

WEBSITES

Garden Organic: www.gardenorganic.org.uk
Permaculture Research Institute: www.permaculturenews.org
RHS: www.rhs.org.uk
Stephanie Hafferty: www.nodighome.com
Vegan Organic Network: www.veganorganic.net

Index

Abies koreana 20
Acer 67, 141
Achillea 60, 212
acidic soil 31, 59
Acmella oleracea 25
Adiantum raddianum 18
aeration 31, 146
Agapanthus 60, 185
Agastache foeniculum 201
Albizia julibrissin 141
Alcea rosea 213
Alchemilla mollis 69, 170,
  202
algae 14
alkaline soil 31, 59
Allium 78, 170
Amelanchier lamarckii 125
Ammi majus 74
Amorphophallus titanum
  25
Anemone 60, 202
angiosperms 21–3
Anigozanthos flavidus 25
annuals 32, 73, 74–6, 170
anther 22, 23
Antirrhinum 72, 136, 142,
  213
aphids 117, 197, 200, 201
Aquilegia 64, 204, 213
Araucaria heterophylla 20
Arbutus unedo 43
aspect 53–4
Asplenium nidus 18
Astilbe 60, 64
Astrantia major 65
Athyrium niponicum 18
aubergine 134, 175
autumn 226–7

balconies 17, 45, 51, 68,
  90–2
  top ten plants for
    98–101
  weight restrictions 91
bamboos 67, 92, 98
bare-rooted plants 32, 56,
  170

heeling in 169
  trees 124, 169
basil 81, 167
bay 101
bedding plants 32, 77
beds 146–50
bees 42–5, 194
beetroot 81, 161
Begonia 69
Bellis perennis 86, 191, 194
berries 40, 44–5, 122, 151
Bidens ferulifolia 205
biennials 32
bird baths 66
birds 40, 42–5, 71, 84, 122,
  151, 198
blueberry 31, 172
bog gardens 60
bolting 34
Borago officinalis 44, 190
borders 53, 82
botanical names 13, 25–30,
  106
botany 14–17
broccoli 81
Brussels sprout 81
Buddleja 144, 216
bulbs 77–8, 118, 148, 170
buying plants 55, 104–17,
  207
  decoding plant labels
    106–9
  seeds 109–10

cacti 99
Caladium 101
Calendula 26, 74, 213
Calibrachoa 72, 136
Calluna 77
Camellia 58
Canna 72, 171
carbon 58
carbon dioxide 16, 84
carrot 79, 134, 150, 174,
  200
Centaurea cyanus 73, 170,
  212

Cercis canadensis 141
Cerinthe major 74
chalk soil 59
Chamaemelum nobile 87
Chelsea chop 214
children 69
chilli pepper 136
chives 166, 200
chloroplasts 16
Chrysanthemum 69, 170
Clarkia amoena 74, 170
clay soil 59
Cleome spinosa 74
climate change 58
climbing plants 52, 88–9
cloches 121, 158
club root 208
coir 61, 153
Coleus 136
colour 51, 68
comfrey 187
common names 25–6, 106
community spaces 41, 113
companion plants 197,
  198, 200
compost 31, 32, 40, 49, 61,
  152–3, 210
  making 217, 218–21
conifers 19–20
containers *See* hanging
  baskets; pots and
  containers
Convallaria majalis 60
coriander 167
corms 170
Cornus 67, 141
Cosmos bipinnatus 74, 170,
  213
courgette 143, 163, 191
Crataegus monogyna 125
Crocosmia 68, 170
Crocus 27, 78, 170
cucumber 175
cultivars 28
Cupressus sempervirens 20
cuttings 94
Cyclamen 60, 77

Dahlia 171
damping off 156, 210
dandelion 188, 194
dead heading 34, 71, 76,
   139, 211–12
deciduous trees and shrubs
   32
Delosperma cooperi 144
Delphinium 170
Dianthus 136
digging 146–7
Digitalis 27, 63, 205, 213
dining areas 68, 90
Dipsacus fullonum 44, 201
diseases 117, 179, 181,
   206–10
dividing, propagation by 34
dormancy 34
double flowers 33
downy mildew 209
drainage 32, 107, 146, 150
drought-tolerant plants 33,
   60, 91, 107, 185
dry soils 60
Dryopteris 18, 60

earthworms 147
Echinacea 132, 170
Echinops bannaticus 45
energy for growth 16
environment 40
Epilobium canum 185
Epimedium 63
epiphytes 33
Equisetum arvense 18, 195
Eremurus 68
ericaceous compost 59, 61,
   172
Erigeron 203
Eryngium bourgatii
   185
Erysimum cheiri 132
established plants 33
Eucomis 78
Euphorbia 204
evergreens 33
exercise, gardening as 38

exotic plants 90
experimentation 50

feeding plants 40, 186–7
   container-grown plants
      139
   homemade fertilizer 139,
      187
   plants in containers 139,
      186–7
fences 52
ferns 17–18
fertilization 22–4
Ficus carica 22, 141
filler plants 33, 71–2
flea beetle 198
fleece, horticultural 140,
   158
flowers 15, 21–4, 40,
   169–71
   edible 188–91
formal gardens 70
formative pruning 214
Forsythia 216
fountains 66
fragrance 29, 44, 45, 67,
   74, 87, 91–2
Freesia 78, 170
Fritillaria meleagris 60
frost 140, 157, 158
fruit 15, 172
   diseases 208–9
   dwarf trees 88, 92, 108,
      141
   grafted trees 107–8
   low-maintenance 79, 81
   planting fruit trees
      122–3, 168–9
   pruning fruit trees 215
Fuchsia 99, 189
full sun 34, 51
fungi 14
fungicides 36
fungus gnat 117

Gaillardia 212
Galium aparine 25

garden size 52
gardening clubs 113
garlic 161, 201, 211
genus 27
Geranium 63, 136, 143
Gerbera jamesonii 132
germination 34
Geum 145, 201
Ginkgo biloba 19, 20
Gladiolus 27, 69, 170, 188
grafted plants 107–8
greenhouses 76, 81, 94–5,
   156, 175
grey mould 209
grow bags 132
grow lights 120
growth 16
gymnosperms 19–20, 21

half-hardy plants 33, 75,
   140
   top five annuals 74
Hamamelis × *intermedia*
   141
hanging baskets 17–18, 52,
   61, 81, 89, 90, 96–7
   overwintering 140
   planting 130, 135–40
   upcycling 137
   watering 135, 138
hard landscaping 55
hardening off 34, 157–8,
   172
hardy plants 33, 75
   top five annuals 74
Hedera helix 42, 69
hedgehogs 40
hedges 44–5, 125, 151,
   214
heeling in 169
Helianthemum 185
Helianthus 69, 170, 189,
   213
Helichrysum bracteatum 74
Helleborus 60, 69, 132
Hemerocallis 68, 142, 190
herbaceous perennials 33

herbicides 36
herbs 82, 88, 96, 164–7, 172
Heuchera 62
Hosta 60, 64
houseplants 18, 61, 120
humus 31
Hyacinthus 78, 170
hybrid plants 28
Hydrangea 59, 98, 170,
216–17
Hylotelephium spectabile
185, 204

Impatiens 136
insects 42–5, 200–1
insect hotels 40, 151,
217
pollinating 22, 24, 40,
73, 86–7, 122, 132–3,
194, 201
Iris 27, 60, 78, 171

Jacaranda mimosifolia 141
Juniperus procumbens 20

kale 81, 134, 160
Kigelia africana 25
Kniphofia 68

labels, decoding 106–9
ladybirds 194, 197
Lathyrus odoratus 120,
154, 212
Lavandula 60, 132, 167,
199
lawns 69, 71, 84–6, 185
chamomile 87
wildflower 84, 86
leaves 14, 15
fallen 147, 221
leek 201, 211
lemon balm 166
lettuce 100
Leucanthemum vulgare 73,
171
lighting schemes 68, 94
Ligularia 60
Lilium 78, 170
loam 59

Lobelia erinus 72, 136
lupin 154
Lychnis coronaria 185
Lythrum salicaria 60

macrame plant hangers 97
Magnolia 58, 141
Mahonia 60
maintenance 70–1, 88
low-maintenance plants
142–5
Malus toringo 141
Malva moschata 171
Mandevilla 100
Mangave 144
Meconopsis betonicifolia 65
medicinal plants 15
Mediterranean-style gardens
60, 90
melon 175
microclimates 34, 54, 89
microgreens 69, 81, 94
Mimosa pudica 25
mint 166
mirrors 94
Miscanthus sinensis 203
moist soils 60, 107
mulch 31, 82, 123, 147,
149, 182, 184, 217, 221
Muscari 78
mushroom compost 61
mustard 81, 100
mycorrhizae fungi 57
Myosotis sylvatica 213

Narcissus 78, 170
Nemesia strumosa compacta
136
Nepeta nervosa 132, 185
Nerium oleander 69
nettle 187, 194
Nicotiana alata 74
Nigella 74, 170, 213
nitrogen 16, 36, 187
no-dig method 34, 128,
146–7, 149, 182
NPK 36, 187
nutrients 14–16, 180

Oenothera lindheimeri 185
Olea europaea 60
onion 80, 175, 209, 211
online forums 114
Ophrys apifera 86
orchid 33
organic gardening 36, 187
organic matter 32, 147
Osteospermum 136, 145
ovary 23–4
overwintering 35
ovule 23–4
oxygen 15, 16, 84

Paeonia 170
Papaver 73, 171, 185
parsley 81, 167
parsnip 174
party areas 68
patents 108
paths 52, 84, 86
patios 52, 53, 68, 71,
88–90
pea 81, 96, 161
peat-free compost 32
peaty soil 59
Pelargonium 92, 136
Pellaea rotundifolia 18
pepper 136, 175
perennials 33, 82, 140,
148, 170, 214, 217
perlite 32
Perovskia 60
Persicaria bistorta 60
pesticides 35, 36, 40
pests 117, 179, 196–205
petals 23
pets 69
Petunia 72, 136, 212
pH, soil 31, 49, 58–9
Phormium 69
phosphorus 16, 36, 187
photosynthesis 14–16
Phyllostachys nigra 67
Picea 20
Pieris 31
pinching out 35
pines 19–20
pistil 23

pizza ovens 68
planning your garden 50–71
plant classification 17
plant families 27
plant hunters 15
plant names 13, 25–30
plant size 52
plant stands 93–4
plant swaps 56, 112
Platycodon grandiflorus 212
plug plants 35, 114, 157, 170, 172
pollinating insects 22, 24, 40, 73, 86–7, 122, 132–3, 194
pollination 22–4
Polystichum setiferum 18
ponds 66, 93, 151
potassium 16, 36, 162, 187
potato 101, 134, 174, 211
pots and containers 52, 55, 115, 131–3, 169
  on balconies 91
  bulb lasagne 77–8
  feeding plants in 139, 186–7
  filler plants 33, 71–2
  green walls 95–7
  herbs for 166–7, 172
  lawns grown in 87
  overwintering 140
  plant stands 93–4
  planting in 130–40
  pollinator plants for 132
  pond buckets 66, 93
  pot-bound plants 35, 116
  recycled 40, 96, 115, 128, 129, 131–3, 152, 155
  siting 53, 92
  size 88
  for small spaces 88, 90, 92–4
  spiller plants 33, 71–2
  strawberries 81
  thriller plants 33, 71–2
  trees for 122–3, 141
  unbreakable 69

vegetable plants for 134
watering 91, 131, 138, 140, 183, 185
wildflower 73
potting compost 61
potting on 156–7
powdery mildew 210
pricking out 156
Primula 60
propagator 120, 156
pruning 35, 82, 119, 179, 213–17
Prunus 125, 141
Pulmonaria 64, 132
Pyracantha 44

QR codes 108

radish 81, 96, 134, 163
raised beds 69, 80, 81, 89, 128–9, 146–50, 169
Ranunculus 86, 170
recycling 40, 55, 76, 96, 115, 118, 121, 131–3, 137, 155
red spider mite 117
respiration 16
rhizomes 171
Rhododendron 31
rhubarb 134, 162
rocket 81, 100
root-bound plants 35, 116
root trainers 120, 121
roots 14–15, 180, 200
rootstock 107–8
Rosa 124, 170, 212
rotivating 146
Rudbeckia 68
runner bean 134, 162
runners 81
rust 210

sacrificial plants 197
salad burnet 167
salad leaves 96, 100, 136, 163
  raised beds 150
Salvia
  S. elegans 190

S. nemorosa 72
S. officinalis 166, 200
S. rosmarinus 69, 199
S. × sylvestris 132
sandy soil 59, 182
Sarcococca 43, 92
scale insect 117
scorch 35
seasonal plantings 139–40
seating 52, 68, 90, 91, 94
Sedum 43, 99
seed compost 61, 76, 152
seed heads 201
seedlings 35
  damping off 210
  hardening off 34, 157–8
  planting out 118, 158
  potting on 156–7
  pricking out 156
  thinning out 35, 79, 159
  transplanting 35
seeds 15, 23–4
  annual 73
  child-friendly 69
  decoding packet descriptions 109–10
  direct sowing 34, 154, 159
  germination 34
  growing from 56, 75–6, 120–1, 129, 148, 152–9, 170
  growing lawns from 84–5
  half-hardy annuals 74–5
  hardy annuals 74–5
  harvesting 40, 56, 76, 212–13
  module trays 120, 121
  sowing 35, 75, 153–6
  succession sowing 35
  watering 65
  wildflower 73
self-seeding plants 33, 76
Senecio candidans 72
sepals 23
sets 80, 175
shade 17, 51, 54, 60, 106–7

dappled 34, 54
deep 34
full 34
introducing 88
part 35
top ten plants for 62–5
sheltered positions 35
shrubs 40, 124, 140, 149,
168–9
fruit bushes 172
pruning 213–17
Silene dioica 73
Skimmia 145
slugs and snails 138,
198–9, 202–5
small spaces 49, 88–97,
125
soil 31–2, 48–9, 57–61,
146–7, 182, 200
compacted 147, 150
soil conditioner 32
Solenostemon 72
Sorbus rosea 125
sourcing plants 104–17
species 27
spermatophytes 21
spiller plants 33, 71–2
spores 18
spring 222–3
spring onion 134
squash 154, 175, 191
Stachys byzantina 185, 205
stamen 23
stem 14, 15
stigma 22–4
strawberry 81, 96, 136, 172
subspecies 28
succulents 99
summer 224–5
sun tolerance 106–7
sunlight 15, 16, 39, 51, 55,
60
full sun 34
sustainability 40
Swiss chard 80, 134
Syringa vulgaris 189

Tagetes 26, 200, 212, 213
Taxus baccata 20

tender perennials 33, 140
Thalictrum 60
thinning out 35, 79, 159
thriller plants 33, 71–2
Thymus vulgaris 132, 198,
199
Tigridia 78
tilth 32
time, planning 70–1, 82–3
tomato 134, 136, 175, 211
tools 118–21, 207
top dressing 32
topsoil 32
*Trachelospermum
jasminoides* 92
trademarks 108
tranquil spaces 66–7
transplanting 35
trees 40, 122–5, 149,
168–9
bare-rooted 124, 169
dwarf 49, 88, 92, 108,
141
fallen leaves 147, 221
for pots and containers
122–3, 141
pruning 213–17
for small spaces 125
Tropaeolum majus 69, 72,
136, 154, 197
tubers 171
Tulipa 69, 78, 170
turf, growing lawns from
85–6

umbellifers 74

variegated plants 35
varieties 28, 106
veganic gardening 36
vegetables 173–5
child-friendly seeds 69
companion plants 200
containers, growing in
134
crop rotation 207
growing from seed
152–9
low-maintenance 79–81

pests and diseases 207–9
raised beds 150
top ten 160–3
Verbena 43, 136
vermiculite 32, 153
vertical space 49, 52, 89,
91, 93, 95–7
Viburnum opulus 45
vine weevil 199
Viola 77
volunteer plants 33

walls, green 52, 89, 95–7
water 14, 16
water butts 56, 184
water features 66–7, 93
watering 40, 56, 71,
180–5, 207
decoding plant labels
107
hanging baskets 135,
138
overwatering 116, 209
pots and containers 131,
138, 140, 183
seeds 65
trees 124, 168
weeds 82, 116–17, 147,
148, 192–5, 207, 219
wellbeing, gardening and
38–9, 58
wild gardens 70
wildflowers 171
in pots 73
wildflower lawns 84, 86
wildlife 40, 86, 93, 151,
192, 194, 201
top ten plants for 42–5
willow 58
wind 91
winter 228–9
wood piles 151

Xerochrysum bracteatum
170

Zantedeschia 60, 171
Zinnia elegans 74, 170, 212

ACKNOWLEDGEMENTS

Huge thanks to the publishing team at Greenfinch for giving me yet another opportunity to spend hours writing about plants, including Katie Crous, Philippa Wilkinson and Julia Shone. Thanks also to: my agent Charlotte Merritt from Andrew Nurnberg Associates International Ltd for guidance; the wonderful illustrator Kaja Kajfež for lifting the pages with gorgeous botanical drawings; and Tokiko Morishima for the perfect layout.

My partner in plants, Michael Perry – thanks for the ridiculously silly messages on a daily basis which really do make me smile, for the book discussions and all-round plant banter.

To my ever-uplifting husband – you are simply the best. Even though I have yet to persuade you to love plants as much as I do, I can see a glimmer of hope. Perhaps this book will be the one to get you gardening! In the meantime, your consistent love and support means everything to me.

First published in Great Britain in 2022 by Greenfinch
An imprint of Quercus Editions Ltd
Carmelite House
50 Victoria Embankment
London
EC4Y 0DZ

An Hachette UK company

A CIP catalogue record for this book is available from the British Library.

HB ISBN 978-1-52942-121-7
eBook ISBN 978-1-52942-122-4

10 9 8 7 6 5 4 3 2 1

Design by Tokiko Morishima
Cover design by Lucy Sykes-Thompson

Printed and bound in China

Papers used by Greenfinch are from well-managed forests and other responsible
sources.